Hear, O Israel

HEAR,
O ISRAEL

A Guide to the Old Testament

James F. Leary

Arena Lettres　　　　　　　　　　New Jersey

Hear, O Israel
by The Reverend James F. Leary

Nihil Obstat: Reverend Kenneth H. Shiner
Imprimatur ✠ John F. Whealon, Archbishop of Hartford

The Nihil Obstat and Imprimatur are official declarations that a book or pamphlet is free from doctrinal or moral error. No implications are contained therein that those who have granted the Nihil Obstat and Imprimatur agree with the contents, opinions or statements expressed.

August 15, 1979

Maps: © United Bible Societies 1976, 1978 "Chronology of the Bible" Chart from the *Good News Bible* with Deuterocanonicals/Apocrypha: © American Bible Society 1979. Used by permission.

Library of Congress Catalog Card Number 80-80627
ISBN: 0-88479-029-0

Contents

CONTENTS

CONTENTS

LIST OF MAPS

Foreword

Father James Leary has, in this book, produced an introduction to the Old Testament that is brief in form but comprehensive in scope. It affords the reader a panoramic view of the Old Testament, from which the Christian Scriptures sprang.

The Christian who is unfamiliar with the Old Testament is spiritually the poorer for that, is at a loss to understand much of the New Testament and misses the significance of many of the readings used in the liturgy. To supply such a person's need is Father Leary's objective.

He succeeds. He is well versed in the sacred writings that detail Salvation History. He conveys his learning simply, clearly and attractively. Under his skillful guidance the reader will see not only the continuity of God's loving dealing with his people in antiquity but also the continuation of that process in their own lives today.

As an aid to mastering the Bible, to greater appreciation of the liturgy and to a more deeply rooted spirituality, Father Leary's book deserves a warm welcome and high praise.

Msgr. John S. Kennedy
Editor, *The Catholic Transcript*

Preface

When the history of this era in Christianity is written, the first three-quarters of the twentieth century may aptly be called the "Age of Biblical Renaissance." Whether it be the popular preaching of a fundamentalist minister on TV, the growth of courses on the Bible at the college level, the faddish "Jesus Movement" among young people or the reemphasis on Scripture in the Church's preaching and teaching, Catholics are aware that in religious circles this is the age of the Bible.

Despite the revitalized emphasis on the Bible, many people find themselves lacking a background from which to read the Scripture. A middle-aged gentleman put his finger on the problem when he said, "With all those references to the Bible in Sunday's homily I feel as if I should take a course in Scripture to decipher what's being said."

The purpose of this book is to answer that need in a modest way by clearly presenting some of the fruits of modern Scripture study in the hope that the reader will encounter material that makes the journey through the Old Testament less formidable and more rewarding.

For the past ten years I have taught courses on the Bible to adult groups, to high school and college students and to graduate students. The experience of these years, especially my interaction with a wide variety of people with an interest in Bible study, has convinced me of the need for basic handbooks that will facilitate the use of Scripture by

PREFACE

the Christian. This book is intended as a guide, a stepping-
stone to the Bible. Obviously, no introduction, regardless
of its quality, can substitute for the actual reading of the
biblical texts themselves. Each believer must allow the
Word of God to touch not only his or her eyes and mind
but, most importantly, the deepest recesses of the heart.

I would like to thank all who encouraged my work,
especially my students at St. Thomas Seminary and St.
Joseph College. I offer my thanks also to Msgr. John S.
Kennedy, editor of *The Catholic Transcript*, for his permission to use some material that originally appeared in
that newspaper. His kind words of introduction and generous help in proofreading the manuscript are both deeply
appreciated. My gratitude is also extended to Elaine
McCarthy, who typed the manuscript. Without her assistance publication would not have been possible.

There remains the agreeable task of dedicating this
work to the memory of my father, James F. Leary, and to
my mother, Myrtle Burr Leary. They introduced me to
Christian faith and constantly encouraged my growth by
their love and sacrifices.

CHRONOLOGY OF THE BIBLE

DATE	
PREHISTORY	**THE BEGINNINGS: EVENTS IN PREHISTORY** Creation Adam and Eve in the Garden Cain and Abel Noah and the Flood The Tower of Babylon
2000 B.C.	**THE ANCESTORS OF THE ISRAELITES** Abraham comes to Palestine. *c.* 1900 Isaac is born to Abraham. Jacob is born to Isaac.
1800 B.C.	Jacob has twelve sons, who become the ancestors of the twelve tribes of Israel. The most prominent of these sons is Joseph, who becomes adviser to the King of Egypt. **THE ISRAELITES IN EGYPT** The descendants of Jacob are enslaved in Egypt. *c.* 1700 — *c.* 1250
1600 B.C.	
1250 B.C.	Moses leads the Israelites out of Egypt. *c.* 1250 The Israelites wander in the wilderness. During this time Moses receives the Law on Mount Sinai. *c.* 1250 — *c.* 1210 **THE CONQUEST AND SETTLEMENT OF CANAAN** Joshua leads the first stage of the invasion of Canaan. *c.* 1210 Israel remains a loose confederation of tribes, and leadership is exercised by heroic figures known as the Judges.
1000 B.C.	**THE UNITED ISRAELITE KINGDOM** Reign of Saul *c.* 1030 — *c.* 1010 Reign of David *c.* 1010 — *c.* 970 Reign of Solomon *c.* 970 — 931

*A circa date is only an approximation. Generally speaking, the earlier the time, the less precise is the dating. From the time of the death of Solomon in 931 B.C. to the Edict of Cyrus in 538 B.C., the dates given are fairly accurate, but even in this epoch a possible error of a year or two must be allowed for.

CHRONOLOGY OF THE BIBLE

THE TWO ISRAELITE KINGDOMS

DATE	JUDAH (Southern Kingdom) Kings	Prophets	ISRAEL (Northern Kingdom) Kings
950 B.C.			
	Rehoboam 931-913		Jeroboam 931-910
	Abijah 913-911		Nadab 910-909
900 B.C.	Asa 911-870		Baasha 909-886
			Elah 886-885
	Jehoshaphat 870-848		Zimri 7 days in 885
			Omri 885-874
		Elijah	Ahab 874-853
850 B.C.	Jehoram 848-841		
	Ahaziah 841		Ahaziah 853-852
	Queen Athaliah 841-835	Elisha	Joram 852-841
			Jehu 841-814
	Joash 835-796		Jehoahaz 814-798
800 B.C.	Amaziah 796-781		Jehoash 798-783
	Uzziah 781-740		
		Jonah	Jeroboam II 783-743
		Amos	
750 B.C.	Jotham 740-736		Zechariah 6 mo. in 743
			Shallum 1 mo. in 743
	Ahaz 736-716	Hosea	Menahem 743-738
		Micah Isaiah	Pekahiah 738-737
			Pekah 737-732
	Hezekiah 716-687		Hoshea 732-723
			Fall of Samaria 722

THE LAST YEARS OF THE KINGDOM OF JUDAH

DATE	JUDAH	Prophets
700 B.C.	Manasseh 687-642	
650 B.C.	Amon 642-640	
	Josiah 640-609	Zephaniah
	Joahaz 3 mo. in 609	Nahum
	Jehoiakim 609-598	Jeremiah
600 B.C.	Jehoiachin 3 mo. in 598	Habakkuk?
	Zedekiah 598-587	Ezekiel
	Fall of Jerusalem July 587 or 586	

CHRONOLOGY OF THE BIBLE

DATE	
550 B.C.	## THE EXILE AND THE RESTORATION

The Jews taken into exile in Babylonia after the fall of Jerusalem

Persian rule begins. 539

Edict of Cyrus allows Jews to return. 538

Foundations of New Temple laid. 520

Restoration of the walls of Jerusalem 445-443

Prophets

Haggai   Zechariah

Obadiah   Daniel

Malachi

Joel?

400 B.C.

THE TIME BETWEEN THE TESTAMENTS

Alexander the Great establishes Greek rule in Palestine. 333

Palestine is ruled by the Ptolemies, descendants of one of Alexander's generals, who had been given the position of ruler over Egypt. 323 to 198

200 B.C.

Palestine is ruled by the Seleucids, descendants of one of Alexander's generals, who had acquired the rule of Syria. 198 to 166

Jewish revolt under Judas Maccabeus reestablishes Jewish independence. Palestine is ruled by Judas' family and descendants, the Hasmoneans. 166 to 63

The Roman general Pompey takes Jerusalem 63 B.C. Palestine is ruled by puppet kings appointed by Rome. One of these is Herod the Great, who rules from 37 B.C. to 4 B.C.

THE TIME OF THE NEW TESTAMENT

A.D. 1

Birth of Jesus*

Ministry of John the Baptist; baptism of Jesus and beginning of his public ministry

A.D. 30

Death and resurrection of Jesus

Conversion of Paul (Saul of Tarsus) *c.* A.D. 37

Ministry of Paul *c.* A.D. 41 to A.D. 65

Final imprisonment of Paul *c.* A.D. 65

*The present era was calculated to begin with the birth of Jesus Christ, that is, in A.D. 1 (A.D. standing for Anno Domini 'in the year of the Lord'). However, the original calculation was later found to be wrong by a few years, so that the birth of Christ took place perhaps about 6 B.C.

I. The World of the Old Testament

THE BIBLE, A FIELD NOT FOREIGN FOR ROMAN CATHOLICS

For the Christian living in the last quarter of the twentieth century and for the ancient Israelite the belief that God communicates with his people has transcended time and culture. Our Jewish and Christian heritage views the Bible as the locus of God's message for us.

There has, no doubt, been an evolution, some would say a revolution, in the Catholic attitude toward the Bible. Perhaps simplistically, the charge used to be made: "Catholics do not read the Bible; after all they have the Pope!" Never, however, has the Church taught that the Bible should be bypassed, although, unfortunately, that was the impression often given. If you think back to the days of your own religious education, you will probably find that a formal study of the Bible was nonexistent.

During the past fifteen years the Bible has played an increasingly important role in the religious education of children and teen-agers. Today, Catholic high schools usually offer a variety of Scripture-related courses. The Bible is an important ingredient in religious studies programs in our colleges. How did the change come about?

A Catholic consensus might indicate that most significant modern-day changes in the Church began with the Second Vatican Council. Actually, there would have been no Council had it not been for the work of theologians and Church leaders of the previous decades who urged the Church to broaden its horizons in many areas. The field of professional Scripture study has seen numerous changes in the past century. Many of its phenomenal advances are incorporated in the documents from the Second Vatican Council.

In 1943, Pope Pius XII issued an encyclical entitled *Divino Afflante Spiritu.* Its point was that, if we want to study the Word of God seriously, we must be aware of the environment that affected its written form. The Holy Father recognized the valuable contribution of Jewish and Protestant Scripture scholars of the nineteenth and twentieth centuries. The spirit of his letter urged Catholics to investigate and build upon their findings.

This document might well be called the Magna Carta of Catholic biblical scholarship. The work of pioneer scholars has now reached the grass-roots level in the churches. At times their findings have seemed a threat to some Christians. Their work has been misrepresented by shock tactics and attention-getting devices. It is, for instance, irresponsible for the homilist to say, "Adam and Eve are mythical people" without providing a solid explanation of what scholars are saying about the first chapters of Genesis. How many parents have been intimidated by a youngster fresh from religion class who pontificates, "There were no Wise Men at Jesus' birth"?

It is to be hoped that the days of sensational reporting and shallow statements are over. The attempt to understand or explain God's Word should not be a threat to a believer. The insights of modern biblical scholars are meant to deepen Christian faith not to demolish it.

One effect of this rebirth of Scripture scholarship has been a deepening of Christian unity. What better place to discover common roots for our faith than in the Bible? Most Christian biblical scholars agree that there is very little of a substantial nature that divides Christian churches in their interpretation of Scripture. The common study of the Bible has been an important milestone on the road to Christian unity.

THE BIBLICAL HISTORY OF SALVATION, OUR OWN JOURNEY OF FAITH

At an adult education program I was asked the question: "If Jesus' message is such a revolution in religious thought, and if the New Testament reflects the essential teachings of Christ, would it not be advisable to reject the Old Testament as part of our Bible and devote our full attention to the New Testament?"

This is not a novel idea. Marcion, (circa 160 A.D.), one of the first Christian heretics, proposed that, since Christianity was a Gospel of Love, the Law of the Old Testament should be excluded from Sacred Scripture. His teachings were rejected by the early Church and the Old Testament today retains its validity for the disciple of Christ.

God's Word is not addressed to us in a vacuum. Jesus' advent in our history was through a Jewish culture and a religious background. He was a pious Jewish believer and, as such, was rooted in the Old Testament traditions of Israel. It is no exaggeration to say that it is impossible to grasp Jesus' teachings without some knowledge of the Old Testament. In Matthew's Gospel Jesus tells us, "Do not think that I have come to do away with the Law of Moses and the teaching of the prophets. I have not come to do away with them, but to give them real meaning" (Matthew 5:17).

As Christians, our faith and religious heritage are grounded in Judaism. In the first decades, the Christians were thought of as one of the many sects within Judaism. All of the leaders of the apostolic church were Jews who carried their Old Testament religious outlook with them as the first Christians. They believed that Jesus had radically altered their relationship with God. However, they never thought that the Jewish scriptures had lost their worth. To insist that the Old Testament is unimportant for contemporary Christians is like saying that the foundation is not essential for the building.

Salvation History is a title frequently given to the Bible. From the first page of the Old Testament to the last word of the New Testament, the Bible represents the story of God saving his people. There is a panorama of God's saving activity on their behalf. "Hesed" is the Old Testament concept for God's loving fidelity to his people. Over and over again the Scriptures make the point that his steadfast love for them endures despite their infidelity and sin.

This Salvation History theme is personified in Jesus' ministry. He stands in perfect continuity with the God of love in the Old Testament, with the God who spoke through his action in human history.

An important dimension of Salvation History is that salvation is an ongoing process. Scripture points to what God has done in our history and indicates what he is doing now and will do for us if we allow his Word to penetrate our hearts.

When we read the story of Abraham, Moses or one of the prophets, it is not merely the history of a religious leader out of the past; it is our story. The faith and faithlessness of ancient Israel is the narrative of our own struggles to believe. The tale of the first man and woman is the story of every person who will ever live. You and I, like Adam and Eve, find that we choose sin over goodness. We, like them, come face to face with God's demands tempered with his understanding forgiveness.

As believers we cannot read any section of the Bible as disinterested observers: The Word of God is the source of our faith in the person of Jesus. The Lord is acting in our personal histories just as he touched the lives of the biblical personalities.

Christians often find the reading of the Old Testament confusing and difficult. Because of their familiarity with the Gospels, their reflection on Scripture frequently stops with the New Testament. Yet, if we put the effort into a study of the Old Testament, the quality of our faith insights will be richer, our appreciation of God's steadfast love will grow and our knowledge of Jesus as the Word will mature.

As we read the Old Testament we encounter difficulty because of a language and cultural gap that is even wider than the one that separates us from the New Testament era. The Old Testament authors spoke to a Semitic people whose thought and speech patterns were far removed from ours.

It is important that we be cognizant of the literary forms that are used in the Bible. As Pope Pius XII reminded us: It is necessary to investigate the environment in which the Word of God is addressed to us.

INSPIRATION,
THE DIVINE QUALITY IN SCRIPTURE

Christians and Jews believe that our God has communicated with us in history. This concept of revelation is important because it makes sense of Salvation History.

Without divine revelation our faith is groundless. In the Bible we encounter a unique evidence of God's communication with us. The Second Vatican Council tells us: "The books of Scripture, firmly, faithfully, and without error, teach that truth which God, for the sake of our salvation, wished to see confided to the sacred Scripture" (Constitution on Divine Revelation, Article 11).

In speaking of inspiration, the Council teaches that God guided the complex process by which the Bible came to us so that Scripture would faithfully reflect his Word spoken in human history.

There are four essential elements in our belief that the Bible is divinely inspired:

1. The impulse to write what is contained in Scripture has its origin in God.

2. The Bible contains what God wishes us to know about him; however, Scripture does not exhaust everything that can be known about God.

3. The human authors were influenced by God in their writing, but not in such a way that they became puppets; human freedom of expression is not obliterated by inspiration.

4. Included in inspiration is God's divine guidance of his people as they selected those writings that would be included in the final version of the Bible.

We would be unfaithful to the third point if we were to describe the process of inspiration as some sort of divine dictation. To say that God dictated the Scriptures word for word, while stressing the importance of God's role, almost makes the Bible seem a book that fell ready-made from heaven. This explanation is too simplistic.

Most contemporary theologians stress the importance of

the community in the formation of Scripture. Rather than speaking of God's working through one individual, it is preferable to think of him as speaking in the community of Israel and in the Church. The individual who writes captures the faith of the people of God.

The word *Bible* means "books." It is a collection of many books that reflect the religious thought, the cultures and the history of well over 2,000 years. It might be better to think of the Bible as a library rather than as a single volume. In its pages we find prayers, songs, battle chronicles, myth, epic narrative and many other literary forms. The one common theme uniting these diverse forms is the belief that the God of love speaks through them.

The first evidence of written Scripture dates from the year 1000 B.C., which means that the tradition of Israel was passed on orally for many years, sometimes for centuries, before it was put in written form. It would be unrealistic to expect from the Bible the strict historical accuracy we have come to expect from modern historians. It is certainly a truthful witness to God's saving activity in our history, but it also contains the human element, which makes it subject to the thought patterns of the era in which it was written.

The people who wrote the Old Testament were products of their time. They were unsophisticated, hardly comparable to the advanced civilizations that surrounded them. For that reason, we must make a sincere effort to adjust to the mentality of its time whenever we read the Old Testament. Our prime concern should be to discover what the author was trying to say and how we can best grasp the ideas for our culture and environment. This process of interpretation is called hermeneutics. The most obvious example is the homily based on the Scripture readings at Mass.

The literalist or fundamentalist reads the Bible in a static framework. He or she fails to recognize the communitarian nature of inspiration and the variety of literary forms found in Scripture. No one would dream of interpreting a love song, an editorial or a politician's campaign speech in exactly the same manner.

We must be tuned in to the spirit and mentality of the literary form if we are to discover the full and accurate meaning of anything we read. If we fail to apply this principle to the interpretation of the Bible we do a disservice to man's role in inspiration.

The Bible is one book in that it has one purpose: to speak God's Word to his people. It is many books in that it reflects the work of many authors, diverse customs and different needs of the faith community.

THE DIVISION OF THE OLD TESTAMENT

Written and collected under divine guidance, the Old Testament represents the literature of God's Chosen People. The word *testament* refers to a covenant or treaty that God made with his people. For Israel, the covenant relationship symbolized God's steadfast love and the pledge of the people to keep faith with the one, true God. Appropriately, the whole history of Israel is explained in terms of the Covenant; that is, Scripture portrays a God who is faithful as contrasted with a people who often turned from his covenant.

Christians believe that, in Christ, a new covenant between God and his people has been formed. The New Testament represents the fulfillment of that first covenant with ancient Israel. Through the life, death and resurrection of Jesus our relationship with God has been radically

altered. But, at the same time, we are heirs of the Old
Covenant. The Old Testament is, for the Christian, a contact with the roots of faith. To better study it, we can divide
the books into several groups.

The Torah

The first major division of the Old Testament, which consists of the first five books, is named in Hebrew *Torah*. Best
translated as "Law," the Torah is especially sacred because
it reflects the traditions of Moses, the founder of Hebrew
religion and law. Israelites thought that Moses was the
author of this section of Scripture. Today some scholars tell
us that these books did not begin to achieve written form
until more than 300 years after Moses' death.

Sometimes referred to by their Greek title, Pentateuch,
these books are the foundation of the Old Testament. Torah
does not mean Law in the juridic sense only. The Hebrew
concept of Torah was much broader than a series of pro-
hibitions. For the Hebrew, God's law represented his guidance and protection in all areas of his people's lives. Without Torah, man would cease to exist.

Genesis, the first book, narrates the creation stories and
presents the Patriarchs as the family history of the Hebrews. Exodus, with Moses as its hero, dramatically gives
an account of the escape from Egypt and the journey to the
Promised Land. Central to it is the covenant made between
God and Moses at Mount Sinai.

Leviticus contains detailed descriptions of cultic ceremonies and deals chiefly with the priests in Israel. Called
by a Hebrew word that means "in the wilderness," the
book of Numbers tells of the journey of Israel to the borders
of Canaan, their Promised Land. (Our English title for this
book derives from a census of the Israelites.)

Lastly, the book of Deuteronomy is a recapitulation of the law of Moses, mostly in the form of his farewell speeches. It stresses that God's people will succeed if they are faithful to the Mosaic covenant.

The Prophets

The second major division of Old Testament literature is called Prophets. It is subdivided into Former and Latter Prophets. The books called Former Prophets do not deal with prophets in the classical sense. They are those of Joshua, Judges, I Samuel, II Samuel, I Kings and II Kings. It is this literature that traces the evolution of Israel from the tribal stage into a mighty nation. Joshua and Judges witness the conquest of Canaan. In I and II Samuel the monarchy is established under Saul and David. Dwelling on the reign of Solomon and his successors, I and II Kings show the tragic results of an oppression of the poor in Israel which undermined the Mosaic covenant. In II Kings, the prophet Elijah appears to call Israel from the midst of paganism to a return to faithful service of the Lord.

The Latter Prophets are said to be the writings of the classical prophets of Israel. Isaiah, Jeremiah and Ezekiel are the longest books and are called the Major Prophets. In addition, there are twelve Minor Prophets. These books are termed "Minor" not because they are unimportant but because they are relatively short.

Prophecy represents a highpoint in the religion of Israel. As men of courage, the prophets challenged Israel to return to the faith of the age of Moses. Standing firm against the inroads of paganism, they inveighed against the corruption of an elitist society that had developed in Israel. Jesus echoed their sentiments when he said that love of God and neighbor is the fulfillment of the covenant.

The Writings

The last major grouping has the general title The Writings. Its books are more philosophical than theological in tone. Most of the literature follows the theme of Wisdom. Man grapples with the mystery of life and its relationship to faith in God. Perhaps less familiar are the books of Proverbs, Qoheleth and Job. Reading them, we become aware that our faith difficulties are not original. Like us, the ancient Israelites struggled to relate their faith in the Lord to the problems and trials of everyday life.

THE HISTORICAL BACKDROP FOR THE OLD TESTAMENT

Most nations can point to one single event or series of events that constitute the beginning of their history. In America's bicentennial celebrations, for instance, we remembered the events in 1776 that initiated the history of the country.

Ancient Israel looked to one decisive event that gave it birth as a people, a nation and a religion. It was the Exodus, the escape of the Hebrew people from captivity in Egypt. All that preceded it, especially the stories of the patriarchs—Abraham, Isaac, Jacob and Joseph—falls into the realm of prehistory. The people of the Old Testament times treated the age of the patriarchs in much the same way as Americans incorporate the events of our colonial period as part of our history.

Sometime between 1250 B.C. and 1230 B.C., the Hebrews ended a long period of servitude in Egypt and, as the Book of Exodus tells us, made good their escape under the leadership of Moses. After forty years of wandering in the wilderness of Sinai, they set out to conquer the land of the Canaanites, their Promised Land. The importance of the Exodus cannot be overstated. It marks the beginning of a covenant between God and the people of Israel, a covenant that continues to this day.

For Jewish people the freedom of the Exodus is still celebrated each year in the rituals of Passover.

Just before the people entered their land of promise, Moses died. Their new leader, Joshua, directed the conquest of Canaan. After it, the Hebrews began to settle in their new land, where government was chiefly tribal in form. Israel was ruled by the Judges, each a brave and charismatic ruler who led her during a time of crisis and then disappeared.

Israel's government evolved to a stronger, more centralized form during the era of the monarchy. In about 1030 B.C. Saul was anointed its first king. He and his successor, David, eliminated the threat from Israel's Philistine invaders.

David died in 970 B.C. and his son, Solomon, inherited a kingdom that soon became one of the great powers of the day. King Solomon made Jerusalem a showplace of the world. Its imposing temple proved to be more a monument to his own grandeur than a place of sincere worship. His callous disregard for the poor and excessive taxation left Israel on the verge of revolt. Shortly after his death Israel was in the grips of a civil war.

Solomon's son, Rehoboam, continued his father's harsh and cruel policies. A rebellion, lead by Jeroboam, set up a rival nation in the northern area of Palestine. Named Israel or Samaria, it continued in existence from 922 B.C. to 721 B.C., when it was conquered by the Assyrians.

The southern kingdom was called Judah. It retained the city of David, Jerusalem, as its capital. Judah survived as an independent state until 587 B.C., when Babylon con-

quered Jerusalem. The time of Israel's kingdom with its
political successes was over.

The next period of Old Testament history is called the
Exile. This refers to 587 B.C. to 538 B.C., when the elite of
Judah were held captive in Babylon. It was a time for the
Jews to rethink their covenant relationship with the Lord.
They gradually came to the awareness that the destiny of
the People of God was not political but religious. In
538 B.C., the Persian king, Cyrus, ended the Exile when he
issued an edict that allowed the Jews to return.

During the years of the divided kingdom and on into
the postexilic times, the prophets were active in Israel.
These heroic men constantly called the people back to
fidelity to their covenant with the Lord. They warned of
the paganistic dangers and reminded the people that love
for God is measured by love for others. Unfortunately, it
was only when the two nations were in ruins that the message of the prophets was heeded.

After 538 B.C., those living in Palestine were victims of
political power struggles. When the Greek empire eclipsed
the Persian dominion, the Jews were subjected to Hellin-
ization. By 167 B.C. they were so outraged by the paganism
being forced on them that they rebelled. A holy war, the
Maccabean Revolt, almost drove the Greeks out of Palestine. It was not until 63 B.C., however, that the Greek period
ended. It was in that year that the Roman general Pompey
captured Jerusalem and Palestine became part of the Roman Empire.

VARIOUS TRADITIONS ENRICH THE
TORAH

When the reader approaches the first five books of the Old
Testament, he or she is aware that this is a different, even

strange, world. A rich variety in literary style becomes evident even to the most casual reader. Inconsistencies abound and the same event is often reported in two or three different manners.

There are two accounts of Creation: Genesis 1 and 2; two versions of the Commandments: Exodus 20 and Deuteronomy 5. The rejection of Sarah's slave girl is reported in Genesis 16 and 21. There are accounts of God's gift of manna and quail to the wandering Hebrews in both Exodus 16 and Numbers 11.

Three times a patriarch attempts to pass off his wife as his sister (Abraham; Genesis 12:10–20 and 20; and Isaac, Genesis 26:6–11). It seems that the story of the Deluge in Genesis 6–9 indicates that several versions of the tale originally existed independently and have been blended to form the account as we now have it. These are but a few of the problems that scholars have attempted to treat during the past two centuries.

From ancient days, there had been a strong tradition that Moses was the author of the Pentateuch. The difficulties with this position have surfaced many times. How does one explain that Moses wrote his own obituary (Deuteronomy 34:5–12)? There are many anachronisms in the Torah, which mentions places and persons that were nonexistent or unknown in the days of Moses.

In Exodus and Deuteronomy, third-person references to Moses are the rule rather than the exception. The highly questionable nature of Mosaic authorship, together with the vastly different literary styles exhibited in the Torah, have led scholars to investigate the possibility that several sources may have been reworked to form the Torah as we have it today.

Scripture scholars owe a debt of gratitude to a German exegete, Julius Wellhausen (1844–1918), who built on the work of his predecessors and gave us the names of four major traditions that lie behind the Pentateuch. Wellhausen's theories have been criticized and reformulated by other experts and today we are able to deal intelligently with the diverse theologies found in the Pentateuch. Commentators on the Bible refer to four basic sources by the letters *J, E, D* and *P*.

Yahwist. The *J* Source takes its name from the German word for Yahweh, God's sacred name in the Hebrew language. It is the oldest of the sources, probably the first that came to written form, in 950 B.C. The tradition behind it reflects its origins in Judah, the southern kingdom. Its language is colorful and the folk narrative style is human and personal. God is spoken of as if he had human qualities.

God's talking with Adam in the cool evening of Eden (Genesis 3:8–10) is typical of the Yahwist. The J material forms the basic core of Genesis, Exodus and Numbers. In these books, God's promise to man is threatened with failure but, at the opportune time, he triumphs once again in man's history and vindicates his promises.

Elohist. Elohim is another Hebrew name for God. From it we derive the *E* Source. First written about 850 B.C., it reflects the traditions associated with the northern kingdom, Israel. Its conception of God is less anthropomorphic: God speaks to men through the media of angels and dreams.

The E tradition is more insular than the J in that there is more concern for the people of Israel and a growing distrust for the surrounding pagan world. The near sacrifice of Isaac by his father, Abraham, illustrates well the dramatic and sensitive characteristics of the E Source (Genesis 22:1–19).

Deuteronomic. The book of Deuteronomy gives its name to the third source, *D* or Deuteronomic. Its first written form appeared about 650 B.C. It is limited almost entirely to the book of Deuteronomy. Theologically, the D Source emphasizes that fidelity to God's law is the key to success for the People of God.

Like the E, it is a product of the northern kingdom. The beautiful confession of faith in the one God of Israel found in Deuteronomy 6:4–9 represents a high point of Old Testament theology and typifies the D document.

(5) *Priestly.* The last source, because of its distinctive interest in the cult and the priesthood, is called the Priestly or *P* Source. It achieved written form in the southern kingdom in about 600 B.C. Practically the whole book of Leviticus is marked by the P Source. It is characterized by precise interest in chronological detail. Lengthy genealogical listings are apparent in it. Genesis 1, with its six days of creation followed by a day of rest, reflects P's interest in Sabbath observance.

The working hypothesis of four sources behind the Pentateuch does not solve all the complex problems that arise when we consider the process whereby the first five books received their final form. The theory does serve to remind us that several diverse theological viewpoints produced the final product we call the Torah. Each of these sources enriched and augmented the other, so that our knowledge of God has grown. A constant theme of all four is that the God of Israel has intervened in our history to save us.

This chapter has outlined some background material that will be helpful to the Christian as he or she approaches the Old Testament. With it in mind, we can begin our journey with the People of God, using the texts of the Bible.

II. Beginnings: Israel's Prehistory

A MEDITATION ON THE HUMAN CONDITION (GENESIS 1–11)

If one were to select the section of the Old Testament that is familiar to most people—and at the same time is the most controversial and misunderstood—it would be the first two chapters of Genesis. They record the primeval history of the Hebrew people. Here we find ancient authors journeying to the dawn of time and drawing out its faith dimension. To read these chapters as if they were an historical narrative would diminish the depth and richness of their meaning.

All ancient people had stories about their beginnings. These often reflected the self-image of the group who wrote them. The origin myths of ancient people frequently give us an idea of their conception of God. Valuable insights into Hebrew faith are found in the first chapters of the Bible.

Two different accounts of creation are found in Genesis. The older begins at Genesis 2:4. It reflects the Yahwist document, with its simple anthropomorphic descriptions of God. Man is pictured in a state of idyllic happiness and living in his garden of Eden.

Genesis 1–2:3, which is influenced by the priestly document, originated later. It is a more stylized account. It is more complex in structure and features the six days of creation, followed by a day of rest, the Sabbath. Both accounts are artists' or poets' conceptions of creation. They were not intended to be historical accounts of the world's beginnings.

When we study the ancient pagan creation myths of Babylonian civilization, it is evident that there are striking parallels to the Genesis accounts. Evidently, it was while the Israelites were exiles in Babylon in the sixth century, B.C., that the Genesis creation accounts were formulated. Although they speak of primal times, they reflect some of the latest Old Testament literature to achieve written form. Perhaps the ancient authors intended these chapters, written in reaction to the Babylonian myths, to stand as a preface to Salvation History.

Although many elements in the creation stories were borrowed from other ancient myths, there are significant differences. Most of the creation myths of antiquity featured an antagonism between the gods and their creatures. Men lived in fear of the capricious will of their gods. Several of these myths indicate that creation was an accident, resulting from a battle fought among rival gods.

In contrast, Genesis tells us that creation is ordered and planned. The God of the Old Testament creates, motivated by his desire to share life with his creatures. In a polytheistic environment, the Genesis stories stress that God is one. He is not a vague force that controls our destinies but, rather, a person, a father, who creates and sustains us because of his love for us.

Man's self-image is enhanced in the Genesis creation accounts. God and man share in the work of creation. Man's naming of the animals indicates his dominance over lower forms of life and the protective care he should exercise on their behalf.

In Genesis, man is the steward of God's creation. A powerful argument in favor of ecology is contained in its first chapters. Man is a creature who has a special dignity. It is only he who is created in God's image, only he who shares God's breath of life.

Genesis stresses the dignity of women. In the midst of a society that thought of her as inferior to man, it strongly asserted the unique role and personality of woman. For its era in history, it is in the forefront in advocating the equality of women and men.

Marriage has a special dignity as a human institution. Genesis speaks of marriage as a loving, caring union between man and woman. It advocates monogamous marriage in the midst of the polygamy and teaches powerful lessons concerning human sexuality viewed in the context of mutual love.

The world-view of Genesis is foreign to us. The cosmology does not square with our modern scientific insights. Hebrews thought of the world as a flat, disc-like surface. It was covered by a dome, called the firmament. Above the firmament were the waters, which would descend through the firmament to the earth. The sun, moon and stars were ornaments hanging in the firmament. Genesis pictures God's creative activity in this framework.

Genesis is not a scientific or historical account of our origins. It reflects an antiquated scientific and world view. There was a time when people who read the Bible thought that evolution was a theory from science that threatened their faith in God as Creator. Today the theory of evolution must be evaluated for its scientific not its biblical merits.

For the believer, it is imperative to move beyond the science and world-view of Genesis in order to discover its theological lessons. Rather than spend time arguing whether or not Genesis is historically or scientifically accurate, the faith community would be better served if we took seriously the messages of belief.

God is a person who loves all his creatures. All people have a special dignity and share his life. We cannot exclude any person from our care and concern. Creation is for man's use, not abuse. Marriage is a sacred relationship between man and woman. Woman has a special dignity and status on a par with her husband's. Each partner complements the other in a relationship cemented by love. These are some of the faith lessons that the opening chapters of the Bible teach and challenge us to live.

Genesis' Creation accounts end on a note of primal innocence: "The man and his wife were both naked, and were not ashamed" (Genesis 2:25). As the serpent enters the picture in chapter 3, the human frailty of the couple becomes accentuated until it leads to their eventual sin and shame.

The poetic genius behind these first chapters of Genesis has cast the serpent in the role of the "heavy." Most of Israel's neighbors deified the snake. Some practiced orgiastic snake worship. In Genesis, the snake became the symbol for all those evil forces in our environment that threaten our commitment to the Lord.

After being seduced by the serpent, Eve shares her disobedience with her husband and bids him eat of the forbidden fruit. This sin episode represents a commentary on Original Sin as the basic condition of humankind. It is not intended to be an exact description of the individual sin of one couple.

All of us can relate to Adam and Eve as they share quilt and become aware of the consequences of their decision. Notice that when the Lord confronts Adam with his sin,

Adam's first reaction is to blame Eve who, in turn, points to the snake. Human nature has changed very little. The age-old inclination to "pass the buck" is evident in the first pages of the Bible.

Due to their misuse of human freedom, the first couple began to experience the effects of sin. Their nakedness became a source of shame as their time of bliss came to a crashing climax. But even amid the disastrous effects of sin a ray of hope glimmered. As a sign of his protective love, the Lord made simple garments to clothe Adam and Eve (Genesis 3:21).

Etiology, an ancient literary form, appears in Genesis 3:14–19. As God orders Adam and Eve from Eden, various human ills originate. Etiology attempts to assign causes for commonplace occurrences in life. For example, a woman's pain during childbirth and the fact of death are attributed as a punishment for the disobedience of the first couple.

The Tower of Babel story in Genesis 11 contains two major etiologies, the explanation of the many different languages spoken by the family of man and a reason for the presence of people in remote areas of the earth.

Evidence that this section of the Scriptures is related to Babylon is found in Genesis 3:24, where the Lord places the Cherubim to guard the Tree of Life. The Cherubim were bull-like statues that adorned the public buildings in Babylon. Their original purpose was to keep away evil spirts and to frighten would-be intruders. The stone lions outside many of our public buildings may well be their descendants. The Cherubim are one of many indications that this section of Genesis was written by a people familiar with and influenced by Babylonian society and customs.

Chapter 4 continues the illustration of sin's effects with an evidence of fratricide in the first family. The feud between Cain and Abel reflects ancient hostility between farmers and nomadic shepherds. Although Abel is murdered, he is the hero of the story. His name, meaning "God is my father," testifies to the author's prejudice in favor of nomadic life. The story of Cain and Abel is set in a time when the world was populated and civilization had advanced tremendously over its status in the previous chapters.

The fantastically long ages attributed to the ancient people should not be taken in a literal fashion. It was probably the intention of the author to show that, as sin increased, the life spans of people decreased. Frequently, a long life span was a way of commenting on the goodness of a person who was supposed to have lived hundreds of years. Methuselah, with his 969 years, still fascinates the reader of Genesis.

The strange story of the Sons of Heaven and the Daughters of Earth, found in Genesis 6, is used as a prelude to the story of the Deluge. Most likely, an ancient myth has been employed to illustrate the experience of the mixture of good and evil in life. Noah is the hero of the Flood and becomes the vehicle for continuing God's promise to his people.

In the Flood, God reacts to man's sin, and yet he works to save a remnant of the people so that his love will continue on earth. Noah's covenant with the Lord (Genesis 9) stresses the very special relationship between the human family and the Lord. There is a mutual exchange of promises of fidelity and the rainbow becomes a tangible witness of the first covenant between mankind and God. Chapter 9 concludes with another etiology as Noah discovers the intoxicating qualities of grapes.

Reflecting on the ruins of an ancient ziggurat, or steppyramid, the author teaches that alienation and guilt result from man's selfish grab for power. The Tower of Babel episode points to man's arrogant attitude before God. The Tower and Flood stories are symbols of a ruined world order. Man has corrupted and polluted the earth by his irresponsible use of his freedom. Chapter 11 concludes with the introduction of Abraham. Through him God will continue his saving work among us.

When we are studying Genesis 1–11, the question "How did it happen?" cannot validly be asked. Genesis is not intended to yield historical accuracy concerning the events related. For the person of faith the important question is: "What are these tales teaching me about God and about my relation to him and the whole human family?"

THE ERA OF THE PATRIARCHS
(GENESIS 12–50)

Every people has had founding fathers to whom legendary and heroic achievements have been attributed. The Hebrews were no exception. Beginning at chapter 12 of Genesis and continuing to the end of the book, the authors introduce us to Israel's heroes in faith. This section of the Old Testament encompasses the tales of the Patriarchs, Abraham, Isaac, Jacob and Joseph. Through a long and complex history of transmission, a folklore with a basis in history has come to us. The stories are valuable because they contain several powerful faith-lessons that have a timeless quality.

The era of the Patriarchs spans the years from 1900 to 1500 B.C. This period is known by archaeologists as the Middle Bronze Age because of the characteristic metal products found among its artifacts.

From the tip of the Persian Gulf throughout the Middle Eastern lands, it was a period of great migration. Tribes were born and some nations passed out of existence. Abraham's migration from Ur of the Chaldeans, to Haran and then to Canaan is typical of the wanderings of desert sheiks of the period. There is one important difference—Abraham's journey was inspired and guided by his God.

Findings of research historians do not prove the existence of the Patriarchs, but much information has recently been unearthed that sheds light on the period into which the Patriarchs seem to fit. It was a time of little stability in which a strong sense of community allowed the survival of certain tribes and in which the lack of community was the death knell of others. No one survives alone in the desert. Hospitality was proverbial among these people.

No actual complex law codes had yet developed. The principle of blood vengeance often settled disputes and justice was swift and, most frequently, cruel. Alliances were sometimes made by marriage, and polygamy was commonplace. Primitive pacts or alliances were made by shedding blood as a token of fidelity. There are several examples of blood covenants in the stories of the Patriarchs.

The natural way for these people to preserve their history was in folk stories. The evening campfire provided the opportunity for the early bards to retell their stories from memory. They form the core of Genesis 12–50, and the chapters were written long after the era of the Patriarchs had ended. What we have come to accept as unique to Abraham and the Hebrew people is, to a large extent, the common folklore of the ancient Middle East. Stories have been adapted to fit Israel's unique understanding of God. The Lord of Israel is a living God who is not material and is utterly transcendent. Yet, he exhibits a special care for his people and enters into a loving relationship with Israel. This belief colors the narrative of the Patriarchs from beginning to end.

Genesis gives an insight into the religious life of the

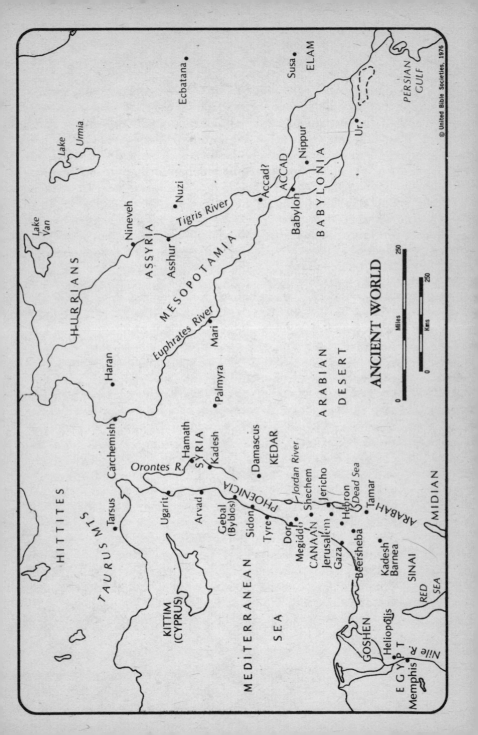

patriarchal period. God was conceived as the patron of the Hebrew family. Unlike many of their neighbors, the Hebrews believed that their God was not confined to any particular place.

Most ancient people thought that each particular area had its own god. When a family migrated from one place to another it usually switched allegiance to the god of the new territory. The God of Abraham, Isaac, Jacob and Joseph was mobile. At this time the Hebrews were relative monotheists. They did not rule out the existence of other gods: rather, they believed that their God was superior to all other gods into whose territory they traveled.

This important belief made possible the survival of their religion. Looking back on history, the biblical authors recognized that the God who guided Abraham across the desert, the God who led Joseph and his family into Egypt and the God who called Moses to be the champion of Israel in the Exodus was one and the same deity.

A recurrent theme in these patriarchal narratives is that through the Hebrews all the families of the earth will be blessed. God chose the Hebrews not because of any special merit on their part but so that his steadfast love might be manifest through them.

With the Patriarchs, God entered into a special covenant relationship with his people. They promised to worship him alone and he promised to protect them and keep them alive as his special family. In this marvelous mystery of election, all things work toward the salvation of mankind through the Hebrews.

God's elective choices still mystify us, just as they did the ancient Hebrews. We are heirs of the promises made to Abraham, Isaac, Jacob and Joseph. We, like they, are called by the Lord to be a people responsible for bringing salvation to all the peoples of the earth.

The stories of the individuals upon whom the patriarchal narratives are built provide food for meditation on the heroic quality of faith.

Ancient Israel did not draw a sharp distinction between the individual person and the community. Rugged individualism in a nomadic environment made no sense at all. No Hebrew could think of himself or herself apart from the tribal family in which he lived. This close identification of the individual with the group is called "corporate personality."

In the Old Testament an individual frequently represents a whole group of people. Such is the case with the Patriarchs. When we read the stories of Abraham, for example, we are in actual contact with the reflections of the Hebrew people on the meaning of faith.

It is this concept of corporate personality that makes the patriarchal narratives meaningful for the Christian today. We are the heirs of ancient Israel in faith. When we read the tales of its founding fathers we are actually learning something about our own faith commitment. The stories of Abraham, Isaac and Jacob are timeless for the person of faith because they are reflections of every person's struggle to believe and to trust in God.

Abraham

Abraham is introduced in Genesis as a powerful desert sheik living near the tip of the Persian Gulf, in Ur of Chaldea. Under direction from Yahweh, he left the security of his home, journeyed across the desert to Haran in Mesopotamia and finally came to dwell in Canaan, which many centuries later would be the land of Israel.

Genesis portrays the core of Abraham's faith as a trustful confidence that God's promise of a new land would be fulfilled. With only God's word as a guide, Abraham made his journey in faith and came to the Promised Land.

When both Abraham and his wife, Sarah, were elderly, God made another promise. He told Abraham that his descendants would be many and that through his family all the nations of the earth would be blessed. Again, the childless Abraham struggled to believe. According to desert law codes, a man whose wife was barren was permitted to have children by his wife's maid. Acceding to custom, Sarah gave Abraham her slavegirl, Hagar, and Abraham's first child, Ishmael, was born. Later, Sarah herself conceived and gave birth to Isaac. The sometimes cruel desert law now dictated that Hagar and her son were to be dismissed and that Isaac inherit the rights of the first-born son.

In Genesis 17, the ancient Semitic practice of circumcision is given a faith meaning. From now on, the circumcision of Hebrew males would be a sign of the person's participation in the covenant made between Abraham and Yahweh. To this day, Jewish people continue this practice, which titles their male children "sons of the covenant."

The ultimate test of Abraham's faith comes in chapter 22, when God asks him to sacrifice his son, Isaac. Once more, the Patriarch surrendered himself to God's Word and made the terrible journey of faith that brought him to the brink of killing his only son. But then, God's Word spoke to him and prevented the sacrifice.

Ancient Israel retold this story many times to indicate not only the firm quality of Abraham's faith but also to show that Yahweh did not wish human sacrifice as a form of worship. In the Abraham stories we view the faith and morality of Israel in evolution.

Isaac and Jacob

Genesis devotes little space to Isaac. It seems as if he is overshadowed by his father and son. Even the wooing of his wife, Rebekah, which is one of the most charming stories in the Old Testament, is conducted by his father's servant. The quiet character of Isaac makes him an appropriate symbol of the covenant being dependent not so much on human ingenuity as upon the willingness to conform human life to God's plan.

Jacob, the clever son of Isaac, outwitted his father and his brother Esau to become heir of the covenant promises.

Genesis does not attempt to cover up the unattractive side of Jacob's personality. Yet, its stories confirm the theme of divine election: God makes use of whomever he wishes to serve his purposes. In no sense does election depend on human merit. Jacob's twelve sons become the new patriarchs of the twelve tribes of Israel. In a symbol of Jacob's role in the birth of the Chosen People, God changes his name to Israel.

Beneath the surface of the Jacob stories is a bit of international history. The conflicts of Jacob with Esau, the father of the Edomites and with Laban of Aram reflect that the long struggle of Israel with its neighbors, Edom to the south and Aram to the north, is told in folkloric, personalized history.

Abraham, Isaac and Jacob are flesh-and-blood human persons. They stand out in Genesis 12–36 as keys through whom God acts in fidelity to his covenant promise. We cannot afford to read these stories in a detached manner because, as we read them, we are looking in a mirror. The same God who elected these men calls us to a similar journey in trustful faith.

Joseph

Genesis concludes with a series of stories about the folk hero Joseph. Biblical scholars regard this section as the best example of editorship in the book because the biblical author has interestingly integrated diverse material into a single novelette. Around Joseph as a central character revolves a dramatic plot that captures and holds the attention of the reader.

The leading theme is the relationship between the protagonist and his brothers. Unlike the other patriarchal tales, the Joseph story is personal and secular. There is a definite theological thrust to the narrative, but it is kept rather discreetly in the background.

Joseph is a transition figure in Salvation History. Genesis tells of his sale into Egypt, his success in Pharaoh's court and the migration of his family to Egypt. With these events Hebrew tradition explained the end of the patriarchal era and the presence of Hebrews in Egypt at the time of Moses. In a real sense the Joseph narrative prepares for the Exodus, the central event in the Old Testament.

The Joseph story is complex, with a definite Egyptian coloring. In his *Dictionary of the Bible*, John McKenzie writes that it is probable that the tale of Joseph and his brothers is largely a creation of edifying fiction. In it Joseph is the ideal man who, by his generosity and willingness to forgive, upholds family unity and saves Israel from extinction.

Unlike the other patriarchal narratives, in which he constantly intervenes in human affairs, God is seldom mentioned in the Joseph section except as a somewhat remote director of man's destiny. There is a close relationship here to the Wisdom Literature of the Old Testament. More emphasis is placed on Joseph as a model of wisdom than on the covenant or cult. The story exalts the same virtues as did Israel's sages when they instructed youth in self-control, discipline, fear of God, family loyalty and high standards of sexual morality.

Joseph, like Isaac and Jacob, was born of a barren woman. As with his father and grandfather, his birth signaled a divine activity among his people. Immediately after his birth in Haran, the family returned to Canaan, where Joseph grew up as a shepherd boy. His coat of many colors was a symbol of his favored status in the family. Most likely the authors have used details from an Egyptian myth called the "Tale of Two Brothers" to heighten the dramatic effect.

Dreams were considered important in the ancient world. Early in his life Joseph earned a reputation as an interpreter of dreams. His dreams, recorded in chapter 37, engaged the envy of his brothers who made plans to kill him. Instead, he was sold to a band of traders who brought him to Egypt where he was a slave to Potiphar, one of Pharaoh's officers.

Joseph was successful in Potiphar's household. As Genesis speaks of his rise to power, it underscores the theological theme that, for the person favored by God, there is no obstacle that cannot be overcome. Potiphar's wife's attempt to seduce Joseph proved that Joseph was a man of virtue. The incident is not, however, an integral part of the Joseph story and most authors believe that it is borrowed from the "Tale of Two Brothers."

After his wife accused Joseph, Potiphar had him put in prison where his expertise in dream analysis brought him to the attention of Pharaoh. Each time that Joseph's social status improves, the author again reminds us that it is under God's auspices. Joseph proved successful in bringing Egypt through seven years of famine and Pharaoh rewarded him by making him a favorite minister, most likely a vizier.

The fact that a foreigner could rise to such high position in Egypt is explained by the domination of the Hyksos, a group of Semites who ruled Egypt in this era. It was the Hyksos who introduced the chariot to Egypt. The Pharaoh who favored Joseph was probably one of these Hyksos rulers.

Chapter 42 turns to the family of Jacob. Through a series of tests Joseph determines the sincerity of his brothers and the family of Jacob is reconciled. As a sign of his forgiveness, Joseph invites his father, Jacob, and his brothers to Egypt. They settle in Goshen, the delta region where the Nile River meets the Mediterranean Sea. It was an Egyptian custom to allow foreign people to live in Goshen and a nineteenth-century B.C. tomb painting at Beni Hassan shows such a group of nomads seeking admission to Egypt.

Genesis concludes with the family of Jacob living in Egypt. It thereby sets the stage for the Exodus.

An apt summary of the theological message of the Joseph story is found in Genesis 50:20, where Joseph speaks to his brothers, saying: "As for you, you meant evil against me; but God meant it for good to bring it about that many people should be kept alive, as they are today."

For young people, the message of Joseph seems to come home on the record *Joseph and the Amazing Technicolor Dreamcoat*, a musical in the popular idiom written by Webber and Rice, who also were responsible for *Jesus Christ Superstar*.

III. The Formation of Mosaic Faith

THE EXODUS: THE KEY TO HEBREW FAITH (EXODUS 1–20; 31–33)

"Now there arose a new king over Egypt, who did not know Joseph" (Exodus 1:8). With these simple words the book of Exodus explains the change in Egyptian attitude toward the Hebrews that saw them fall from a favored position to one of slavery. Egyptian history indicates that in approximately 1550 B.C. the Pharaoh Ahmoses I expelled the Hyksos from his kingdom. They had been the semitic rulers in Egypt when Joseph and his family settled there. After the expulsion, the semitic people who remained in the delta region were forced into slavery to work on the various building projects undertaken by the dynasty.

There is a large time gap between the closing chapters of Genesis and the beginning of Exodus. No doubt it was sometime during this period that Hebrew bondage in Egypt began. Exodus does not name the Pharaoh who oppressed the Hebrews, but all evidence points to Seti I (1309–1290 B.C.). To him is credited history's first incident of anti-semitism. Most likely the Hebrews served as laborers as the cities of Pithom and Rameses were being constructed in northern Egypt.

Like that of Genesis, the literary construction of Exodus is complex. The text is in the form of a legend and incorporates elements of the Yahwist, Elohist and Priestly sources. Cult played an important part in the formation of the Exodus narrative. Many scholars believe that its first half is an actual cult legend that was retold at Israel's Passover celebrations.

In worship each generation of Israelites re-enacted the Exodus story so that they conceived of themselves as bearing the burdens of slavery and sharing the joys of eventual freedom. To this day, Jewish people relive the events of the Exodus as they observe Passover each year.

The Exodus remains the central event in the Hebrew Scriptures. Without it there would be no land of promise for God's people. The Exodus is the source of Israel's political, social and religious life. No other Old Testament event colors Salvation History as it does.

Moses is the hero of the Exodus. We are told that he was saved from infanticide, adopted by an Egyptian princess and raised as a scribe in the courts of Egypt. As a young man, he killed an Egyptian who was beating a Hebrew slave. As a result, he had to flee from Egypt to the land of Midian in the Sinai peninsula. There he joined a nomadic tribe and founded his own family. While pasturing his father-in-law's flocks, Moses experienced a special awareness of God's presence in his life. Through the medium of the burning bush, God spoke to him and told him to return to Egypt in order that he might lead the Hebrews to freedom.

Initially, Moses was reluctant to heed God's call. In Exodus 3 he was commissioned to introduce the Lord to the Hebrews. The Divine Person was to be known by his sacred name, Yahweh. Gradually, Moses came to the awareness that Yahweh and the God of Abraham, Isaac and Jacob

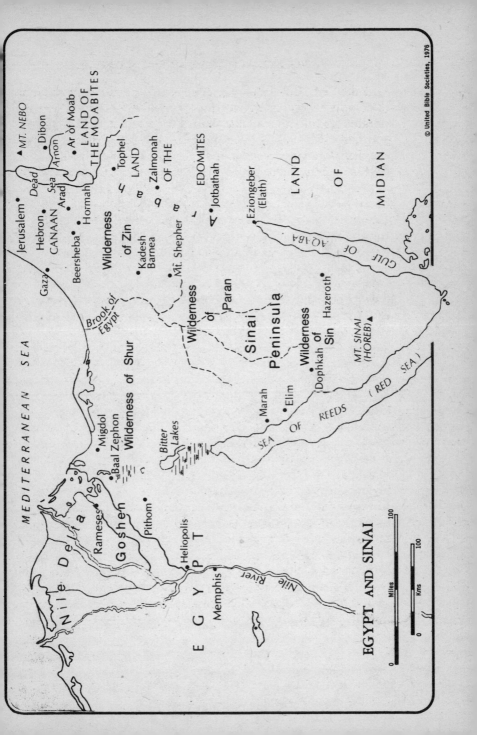

EGYPT AND SINAI

© United Bible Societies, 1976

were one and the same, the Savior of the Hebrews. Equipped with extraordinary power intended to validate him before his people and to win Pharaoh's promise of freedom, Moses returned to Egypt with his brother, Aaron. The Pharaoh whom Moses confronted probably was Rameses II (1290–1224 B.C.).

The dramatic effect increases with a series of plagues visited upon Egypt which are intended to convince the king to free the Hebrews. All of these maladies can be rooted in natural occurrences. For example, plagues of locust and boils were common and spring floods frequently turned the Nile blood-red as they washed clay deposits into the water. The author of Exodus has theologized history, using these natural catastrophes to indicate that Yahweh was working for the salvation of his people.

The last plague brings the death of the first-born Egyptian children. After it Pharaoh capitulates and allows the Hebrews to leave Egypt. Exodus 12 incorporates the story of the first Passover meal. The blood of the Paschal lamb became the symbol of life as the Hebrews were saved from the last plague. When the early Christians spoke of Jesus as "the Lamb of God," it was this section of the Hebrew Scriptures that inspired them. The Passover meal, eaten in haste, prepares both the participant and the reader for the next dramatic intervention of Yahweh.

"Let my people go, that they may serve me." This recurrent theme in Exodus portrays the contest between Moses and Pharaoh. Theologically, the statement attests to the transference of Israel's loyalty from Pharaoh to Yahweh. The narration of the plagues builds on the same theme, namely that God's purpose to save Israel from slavery and to make the Hebrews his ambassadors to the nations will not be thwarted, even by the great powers of the day.

Exodus gives poetic witness to Israel's belief that the

mighty power of Yahweh revivified his people as they fled from Egypt into the wilderness of the Sinai peninsula.

Four different oral traditions have been woven together to form the Exodus account. While the story of the Exodus is based on a historical event, we cannot expect it to yield precise historical detail. Unfortunately, Cecil B. DeMille's film *The Ten Commandments* still tends to color people's thinking.

We must remember that the account of the Exodus, as we find it today, bears the effects of the telling and retelling of the story over many generations. Each age reformed its own traditions about the significance of the Exodus event. In new situations and places different authors found different emphases that made the Exodus event ever-young.

As the reader follows Israel's escape across the sea, he or she is awed by an intense awareness of God's presence with his people. Because of an ancient mistranslation of the text, we have come to associate the body of water that was crossed with the Red Sea. The Hebrew original, however, tells us that the Hebrews escaped through the "Yam Suph," which is best rendered "sea of reeds."

Most likely the crossing of water took place in one of the marshy regions of northeastern Egypt, probably in the area of what is now the Suez Canal. The exact location, however, is rather insignificant. The important point is that the Scriptural traditions all testify that in the hour of supreme need the Lord intervened to deliver his people.

As an event, Exodus is still celebrated today not because it stressed the superiority of the Hebrews as a people but because it exalts the merciful intervention of a loving Father in the history of his children.

Exodus 15 contains a triumphant song praising God for Israel's victory over the Egyptians. This longer version is based on the terse Song of Miriam, Exodus 15:21, which is one of the most ancient fragments preserved in the Old Testament.

After their escape the Israelites journeyed from the Sea of Reeds to Mount Sinai, the site of Moses' first encounter with the Lord. In this wilderness the faith of the Hebrews met its test. It appears God's people were quick to complain and to lose their vision of hope as the various obstacles of desert survival confronted them.

Exodus 13 concludes by indicating that God's guiding presence remained with the Hebrews in the pillar of cloud, which led them during the day, and the pillar of fire, which marked out their path at night. Throughout the Bible, fire and cloud are special symbols of God's love and protection in the lives of his people.

As proof that Yahweh willed the survival of his people, the authors of Exodus indicated that God fed his people as they travelled across the desert. Manna and quail are viewed as his special gifts to the Hebrews.

The remnant of the manna and quail is still found in the Sinai area. Manna is the secretion of several insects that feed on the tamarisk bush. It is a sweet substance which can easily be gathered from the ground. Quail migrate from the Mediterranean areas crossing Sinai on the way to Africa and Arabia. After the long flight the birds are ready-made targets for hunters.

When Israel, under the leadership of Moses, finally arrived at Mount Sinai, her origin and mission again were clarified by Yahweh. Exodus 19–40 combines legend with ancient law. When Moses came to Sinai he once more experienced the presence of God in a vivid way. The narrative of the theophany reminds us of the initial call of Moses in Exodus 3. At Sinai the Mosaic covenant invited God's people to a renewal of friendship with him.

Although the various laws reflect ancient legislation,

much of their content presupposes a settled, agricultural people. As a people of the land, Israel did not emerge until long after the days of Moses.

The ancient Hebrew did not look upon God's covenant law as a set of restrictions that hindered freedom; rather, he viewed the Torah as a sign of God's guiding presence continuing in his life. The Mosaic covenant made Israel sensitive to her responsibilities to God and to mankind. It challenged the Hebrews to a level of social awareness unmatched in the ancient world.

The story of the Golden Calf in Exodus 32 indicates that, even in these peak moments, the faith of Israel faltered. Aaron, the brother of Moses, produced a statue representing an ancient fertility god. When confronted with his idolatry, Aaron offered a pathetic explanation: "They gave it [gold] to me, and I threw it into the fire, and there came out this calf." Lame excuses for sin and lack of trust clearly are not original to us!

With their God and his law to guide them, the Hebrews continued their desert travels until they came to the borders of the Promised Land. But the events of the Exodus remained indelibly imprinted on their collective memory.

THE PASSOVER, A CELEBRATION OF FREEDOM

When a Catholic participates in the liturgy of Holy Week, especially during the Easter Vigil, he or she is immediately aware of the many references to the Jewish feast of Passover. In addition, each gospel writer stressed the Paschal dimensions of Jesus' passion, death and resurrection. An understanding of its Passover roots will be helpful for the Christian who wants to enter into the liturgy and the Scripture of this sacred week.

THE PASSOVER, A CELEBRATION OF FREEDOM

The Passover has been celebrated by Jewish families for many centuries as a memorial of the Exodus event. God's special love and care for his people was printed indelibly upon Hebrew consciousness. As the authors of the Old Testament reflected on the Hebrews' escape from Egypt, it quickly became the focal point of Salvation History.

Most authors believe that the origins of the Passover celebration predate the Exodus. Like many holidays, this festival is rooted in nature. Prehistoric shepherds observed a festival celebrating the birth of the new lambs. It coincided with the full moon in the spring. Families marked the occasion by the sacrifice of a sheep or goat from their flocks. The sacrifice was offered at nightfall and the animal was roasted whole with none of its bones broken. All the members of the family ate a meal in haste at midnight.

The sprinkling of the tent posts with the lamb's blood was an essential part of the observance. Primitive shepherds saw the ritual as a way to ward off plague and illness.

Another celebration that the Hebrews adapted to observe the Exodus was the Canaanite festival of unleavened bread. When they settled in the land of the Canaanites they became an agricultural people. In the spring the people of the area observed a festival marking the grain harvest. During it they ate unleavened bread as a safeguard against an unproductive year. Central to the feast was the offering of the first sheaf of the harvest grain to the gods. People believed that everything on earth belonged to the gods and that man as the steward of creation offered the best of his harvest in gratitude to them.

These two pagan festivals form the historical basis for Israel's Passover. Centuries after the Exodus the Jewish people adapted them to celebrate the origin of their freedom when God delivered them from slavery in Egypt. The memorial of this great event in Israel's history became the chief reason for the celebration of the spring festival. Nature's renewal in the spring and the idea of human freedom coupled to make the Passover a festival of freedom for the Jewish people.

Customs and ceremonies formerly linked with the feast of unleavened bread and the nomadic shepherds' festival have been reinterpreted to become associated with the Exodus as a symbol of the human quest for freedom.

When the Jerusalem Temple was destroyed in A.D. 70, the sacrificial dimension of Passover was lost. Since then it has been mainly a memorial of the saving acts of God in Israel's past. At the same time, it looks to the future, never ceasing to awaken Israel's hope for better times. The parting blessing at the Passover meal is centuries old and is still used today: "Next year in Jerusalem!"

As observed by contemporary Jews, the festival of Passover is introduced by a beautiful family service in the home. The Seder, or order of service, incorporates Israel's precious memory of a saving Lord. It looks to the future with hopeful joy as the time of the fulfillment of his promises. Its principal elements are the unleavened bread, bitter herbs and wine, each of which recalls the sorrows and joys of the Hebrew people.

The theme for the meal is set as the youngest child asks the question: "Why is the night of Passover different from all other nights of the year?" In response the head of the household tells the story of Israel's deliverance with its promise of a redemption that extends beyond the Chosen People.

The service is interlaced with a festive meal and concludes with psalms and popular folk hymns in hopeful anticipation of the coming of God's reign. Just before a final cup of wine is consumed in gratitude for the good gifts of God, the participants say: "On this Festival of Freedom, we pray that liberty will come to all men, that a happy life, peace and contentment will be the possession of all."

Celebrating this freedom meal, the Jew of every age is reminded of his or her responsibility of sharing and insuring the blessings of freedom for all people.

The Christian cannot remain aloof to the celebration of Passover. Early Christian writers, especially those of the New Testament era, associated the Passover with the events surrounding the death and resurrection of Jesus. It is not coincidental that the Last Supper was cast in the form of a Paschal meal. Jesus, shortly before his journey from death to life, ate the Passover with his friends.

For the Christian the Eucharist is a new celebration of freedom. As we share the Lord's Body and Blood, we are mindful of the acts of a loving God in our collective and personal lives. Like the festival of Passover, the Eucharist emphasizes the responsibility we have to insure the freedom of all people.

If we are aware of our Jewish background, we as Christians cannot ignore the social dimensions of the Lord's Supper. As we celebrate the Eucharist, we, too, commit ourselves to work for the freedom of all people so that God's reign may come to completion among us. The Exodus of God's People is more than an event of history; it continues today wherever human freedom is achieved and valued.

THREE BOOKS REFLECTING MOSAIC TRADITION

The Books of Leviticus, Numbers and Deuteronomy complete the Torah. Like Genesis and Exodus, each has its own theological character. Their unique features are presented here only in outline form.

Leviticus

Leviticus can be described as the manual of liturgy for the Jerusalem priests who lived in the post-Exilic period (circa 540 B.C.). A unit of priestly tradition begins at Exodus 25. Leviticus builds on that legislation, embodying the Priestly Source almost entirely.

Leviticus may be divided as follows: (1) chapters 1–7, the laws concerning sacrifice; (2) chapters 8–10, the consecration of priests and their sacred duties; (3) chapters 11–15, laws regarding ritual purity, or Kosher laws; (4) chapter 16, ceremony for the Day of Atonement; (5) chapters 17–26, the Holiness Code, or laws to govern Israel's life as a holy people, and (6) chapter 27, an appendix on religious vows.

Much of the material in Leviticus makes for tedious reading. The first few pages contain detailed instructions about the five main types of animal and grain sacrifices. Some people have misunderstood Israel's notion of sacrifice, relegating it to a primitive, magical means of escaping guilt or insuring the benevolence of the deity. In fact, the Israelites offered sacrifice to God because they experienced a profound realization of Yahweh's holiness and an inner need to relate to him through established ritual sacrifice.

The motivation for sacrifice in Israel was three-fold:

1. It acknowledged God's dominion over all creatures by returning to him a portion of his gifts.
2. It was a means of communication with God.
3. It repaired a covenant relationship.

Israel's theologians were aware of the nearness of God. It convinced them of sin and prompted them to return to him in sacrificial service.

Chapter 16 contains the laws for Yom Kippur, the Day of Atonement. This was the most solemn of all Israel's fasts. It continues to be observed each year in mid-autumn and marks the completion of days of penitence at the beginning of the New Year. During this observance the people's sins were symbolically imposed upon the scapegoat and he was driven into the desert to die. Yom Kippur was the only day on which the High Priest entered the Holy of Holies in the temple.

As we study Leviticus we become aware that this is more than a history of cultic rules. It is a testimony to Israel's belief that God provided the means of atonement and forgiveness; thus the community of faith could be restored to holiness and reconciled with him.

Numbers

The fourth book of the Torah takes its English title from the census at the beginning of the book. In Hebrew it is named by the first word, *Bemidbar* ("in the wilderness"). This designation is more appropriate for the contents of the overall book, which narrates the movement of Israel from Sinai to the borders of Canaan.

Numbers covers the traditional forty years that Israel spent in the desert of Sinai. Much of the book overlaps the end of Exodus and sections of Deuteronomy. It has no real unity; nor does it appear to have been composed according to a logical or predetermined plan. The priestly tradition predominates. There is a marked tendency to retroject into the Mosaic era the laws and institutions of postexilic times.

Moses emerges as an attractive hero who is deeply compassionate and sympathetic to his people even when they betray trust.

Numbers is a testimonial to Yahweh's providential care for his people. He dwells among them in steadfast love. The book stresses that man is bound to obey God and that disobedience is met by divine punishment. God, however, never totally abandoned his people and Numbers assures us that he is attentive to their prayers.

For the sake of study, the book of Numbers may be divided as follows: (1) Chapters 1–10:10, the events at Sinai; (2) Chapters 10:11–21, the journey to Moab and (3) Chapters 23–36, Israel's encampment on the Plains of Moab. It ends with Israel under the leadership of Moses and Joshua preparing to conquer the land of the Canaanites.

Deuteronomy

Deuteronomy, the fifth book of the Torah, takes its name from a Greek word meaning "the second law." It consists mainly of three major speeches of Moses that supposedly were delivered as the Israelites were camped in Moab prior to the conquest of the Promised Land. Its words obviously are not actually those of Moses, yet the thrust of the book is without a doubt Mosaic.

The law is viewed as a sign of God's presence in the hearts of his people. Deuteronomy underscores God's spontaneous, saving choice of Israel. The observance of the law is seen as part of the response of a grateful people. The book's style is distinctive. A pattern of set phrases and oratorical devices recurs constantly. There is a definite sermonic character. Theological themes such as the election of Israel, the importance of observing Law and the confidence in the power of God are emphasized.

Most likely, Deuteronomy received its final form during the reign of King Josiah (640–609 B.C.). This reformer king, influenced by the prophet Jeremiah, promulgated legislation aimed at drawing his people back to a pure Mosaic faith.

Deuteronomy 6:4–5, the famous "Shema" prayer of the Jewish people, emphasizes the attitude of the believer toward his God: "Hear, O Israel: the Lord our God is one Lord; and you shall love the Lord your God with all your heart, and with all your soul, and with all your might."

It is a fitting conclusion to our study of the Torah. It highlights the theology of the first five books of the Old Testament, each of which challenges us to respond to God's saving activity by committing ourselves to the Lord in love.

IV. The Divine Promise Fulfilled

CONQUEST OF THE PROMISED LAND (JOSHUA 1–11; 23–24 AND JUDGES 1:1–2:5)

The Torah concludes with Deuteronomy's description of Moses' death, after he had seen the Promised Land from Mount Nebo. As Moses fades from the biblical scene, a new hero emerges as the leader of the Hebrews. Joshua is the central figure of Israel's conquest of Canaan. The book named in his honor is our chief source of information for this period.

The book of Joshua may be divided into three units: (1) chapters 1–12, the conquest of the Promised Land; (2) chapters 13–22, the division of the land among the tribes of Israel and (3) chapters 23–24, Joshua's farewell speech and the covenant renewal ceremony at Shechem.

The entire book is the work of a Deuteronomic historian and emphasizes many of the same theological themes as Deuteronomy. In Joshua, God's promise of a land for his people becomes a reality. Although it draws a portrait of Joshua that is heroic in nature, its primary theme is that, through the leadership of Joshua, Yahweh continues to work in Israel's history as a Saving Lord.

The book of Joshua begins with the Hebrews encamped on the east side of the Jordan river awaiting the word to attack the land of the Canaanites. Before crossing the river, Joshua sends spies to the city of Jericho. They are aided by Rahab, a prostitute, who is promised safety when the men return to attack her city.

The hour of conquest arrives and Joshua leads his men across the Jordan. Reminiscent of the crossing of the Sea of Reeds, the waters of the river part to allow the army to pass to the other side.

The first Israelite camp in Canaan is set up at Gigal and there the Passover is observed. No doubt the account of these events in Joshua 1–5 bears the marks of editors who heightened the miraculous nature of the march into Canaan in order to stress the fidelity of God who was giving his people their Promised Land.

As recounted in chapter 6, Jericho's conquest never fails to impress its readers with its exciting details. Under the leadership of the priests, the Hebrews surrounded the walls of the city. As they shouted and blew their horns the walls of the fortress collapsed and the army of Israel entered the city.

Present-day moral consciousness may be alarmed by the sacrificial ban of holy war, the *herem*. By this concept all life—human included—was destroyed by the victorious army. Booty and any valuables in Jericho were burned as a sign that the Hebrews gained nothing by their conquest except a place to live.

A nation that obliterated two Japanese cities and fire-bombed peasant villages in Vietnam cannot sit in judgment on ancient Israel. The horrors of war often suspend the moral judgment of its participants.

Archaeological findings do not confirm the wholesale destruction of Jericho around 1200 B.C. Kathleen Kenyon's excavations there indicates that, at the time of the conquest, it was merely an insignificant Canaanite garrison. The reputation of its past greatness and the fact that it was the first site occupied in western Palestine indicates why the destruction of Jericho was narrated in such magnificent detail.

Following the fall of Jericho, Joshua's army moved northwest to conquer the city of Ai. In Hebrew *Ai* means "the ruin." The noted historian of ancient Israel W. F. Albright has proposed that the Hebrews actually conquered the neighboring city of Bethel and that the details of this victory have been transferred to Ai, an obviously ruined city.

When Ai was subdued, the conquest moved to the southern territory. Archaeology confirms that the cities of Lachish and Debir were destroyed at this time. It was during this campaign that Joshua bid the sun stand still so that Israel would have added daylight for the fight (Joshua 10:12–14). This figurative account is the author's way of stressing the importance of Yahweh's sustaining presence for Israel's victory.

Moving from the south, the army conquered most of the northern territory. Joshua 11 concludes with this summary of victory: "So Joshua took the whole land, according to all that the Lord had spoken to Moses." Joshua's division of the land among the tribes of Israel concludes the narrative.

The first two chapters of the book of Judges also contain an account of the Hebrew conquest of Canaan. Joshua is not the central figure in this narrative. In fact, its opening line states that Joshua is dead. Whereas the conquest in Joshua is a quick, lightening-like process, Judges characterizes the invasion as a very slow and gradual takeover of Canaanite territory.

Perhaps the method of conquest witnessed by Judges is

closer to the historical fact. The important theological message of Joshua is not compromised however. It indicates that it was Israel's firm belief that God's promise to her was now fulfilled in the gift of the land.

Joshua's farewell admonitions to Israel (Joshua 23) are followed by a ceremony renewing the covenant at Shechem. Joshua 24 begins with a rehearsal of the wondrous deeds of Yahweh done on behalf of his people from the call of Abraham to the Conquest. The book continues with the request that the people shoudl choose to serve Yahweh rather than the Baals, the Canaanite fertility deities.

The people pledge their fidelity to God: "The Lord our God we will serve, and his voice we will obey" (Joshua 24:24). At the conclusion of the ritual they erect a *massebah*, or stone monument, as a testimony to their covenant promises. By this treaty Mosaic faith was extended to the tribes that had not been part of the Exodus. Israel's decisions to heed or reject this covenant would spell the difference between success and failure in her future.

"WHEN THE JUDGES RULED . . ."
(JUDGES 2:6–16:31)

From the conquest of Canaan, 1200 B.C., until the establishment of a monarchy in Israel, 1020 B.C., the Hebrews were in a period of formation. In this 200-year period Israel evolved from a loose confederation of tribes into a relatively stable form of government.

When the Hebrews occupied Canaan many factors seemed to indicate that their era of dominance would be short-lived. They were a heterogeneous mixture of several peoples, not all of whom traced their roots to the Exodus. The Canaanites were a more sophisticated people with a

developed aristocratic government. There were few crafts-
men among the Hebrews; in fact, there was scant respect
for the amenities of civilization.

Archaeologists distinguish between the fine homes of
the Canaanites and the rustic shacks of the Hebrews. Israel
had little art and probably no music of its own. In contrast,
there is evidence of an intricate liturgical art and music
centering in the Canaanite temples. Canaanite religion developed a rich mythology appropriate for an agricultural
people. The Hebrews worshipped a mobile desert God
whose effectiveness in a farming locale could well be questioned. These and many other factors did not augur a successful future for the Hebrew people in Canaan.

Practically all of our biblical information for this period
comes from the Book of Judges. It reflects an era of bringing
structure out of chaos. Once the Israelites possessed the
land the settling down process began. As growth toward a
centralized power took shape, the Hebrews looked to Yahweh for security.

The Deuteronomic historians who authored Judges
wove their narrative around twelve Judges who ruled Israel
during this period. We must not think of a judge in the
purely juridical sense. *Shofet,* the Hebrew concept, referred to charismatic or spirit-possessed personalities who
arose spontaneously to lead Israel in time of national or
religious crisis. The tribes of Israel were joined in a somewhat unstable confederation united by a common covenant
with Yahweh. This style of tribal government, based on a
common sharing of creed, is called an amphictyony.

Two crucial issues faced the Hebrews in the era of the
Judges. The first had social and national dimensions. Israel
asked herself what would be the nature of her relations
with the original inhabitants of Canaan. In contrast to the
book of Joshua, Judges indicates that there was little con-

flict between these two parties after the initial period of conquest. Israel's decision to preserve its unique social and national identity made it possible for a monarchy to emerge years later.

The second, and more important, issue was a religious one. The Canaanites worshipped the Baals, who were fertility gods. Their religion was essentially a fertility cult linked with the cycle of nature. As the Hebrews settled in Canaan and became an agricultural people, they questioned whether or not Yahweh, a desert God, had jurisdiction in this new land. In times of war they called upon God, who had delivered them from Egypt; but in good times it was tempting for them to fall into the fertility worship of their neighbors.

The Hebrews' decision to preserve the covenant faith in Yahweh meant the survival of monotheism in Israel. The strong temptation to paganism would, however, always be a factor in the faith and faithlessness of God's people.

Throughout the stories of the judges a cyclic pattern is evident. First, Israel is unfaithful to Yahweh by worshipping other gods. Then, God sends his judgment on her sin, usually in the form of an invasion by a hostile tribe. Next, Israel recognizes her sin and calls out to God for mercy and deliverance. Finally, God raises up a judge who rescues Israel from the impending danger.

The process of sin, judgment, repentance and deliverance is repeated again and again in the Deuteronomic conception of history. It is testimony to the belief of the authors that Israel's history disclosed Yahweh's presence in his judgment and his mercy. Hidden forces of human sin and divine judgment were seen to be the source material for historical events.

There were six major judges in Israel: Othniel, Ehud, Deborah and Barak, Gideon, Jephthah and Samson. Perhaps the story of Samson in Judges 13–16 is the most familiar of the narratives. He was the Hebrew Paul Bunyan and his extraordinary feats of strength became legendary. He carried on a singlehanded contest with the Philistines, a seafaring people who were invading the coastlands of Canaan.

Samson is often called the "colossus with the feet of clay" because his violent anger and lustful nature proved his undoing. Under the spell of the Canaanite woman Delilah, he was reduced to an ineffectual weakling. As he lay bound in a Philistine shrine, Samson implored God for a return of his former strength. His request was granted and he performed his final act of vengeance by pulling the temple down on himself and the gloating Philistines.

Samson the hero certainly was not an exemplary character. His morality leaves much to be desired. Yet, his presence as a hero of Israel is in itself testimony to the belief that God worked even through the weak sinners of the world.

The Book of Judges concludes with the words: "In those days there was no king in Israel; every man did what was right in his own eyes" (Judges 21–25). The stage is set for the next step in Israel's development, the beginning of the kingdom.

THE EMERGENCE OF A KINGDOM IN ISRAEL (I SAMUEL 1–16; 27–31, II SAMUEL 1–24 AND I KINGS 1–11)

As a structure for governing Israel the temporary institution of the Judges proved inadequate when the people began to face more sophisticated problems. Confronted with a threat from the Philistines, a danger far more serious than that posed by the remnants of the Canaanites, Israel realized the need for a stronger, more centralized form of government. The serious crisis in leadership began Israel's evolution from a tribal confederacy to a monarchy. Within a century Israel became a political force with which to be reckoned.

Our principal source for information concerning this period is First Samuel, called First Kings in older versions of Catholic bibles. Internal evidence indicates that an editor of First Samuel has combined several varied and at times conflicting sources. One of them views the monarchy as ordained by God for the survival of his people. It reflects the oldest traditions. Examples of its promonarchical character are found in First Samuel 9:1–10:16 and 11:1–15.

Another major source, from a later era, judges the kingship in Israel as a theological mistake. This antimonarchical source is reflected in First Samuel 8:1–22 and 10:17–27. Its author sees Israel's having a human king as an affront to belief in Yahweh, the true king of his people. One of ancient Israel's favorite titles for Yahweh was "King of the Universe."

For the antimonarchical philosophy a human king would compromise Israel's total faith-dependence on her Lord. Those who held this view were quick to point out that under the leadership of Yahweh the Hebrews overcame the power of Egypt and its mighty pharaoh. Would not the power of God be adequate to meet the crisis of the Philistine invasions? The antimonarchical authors were in a "we told you so" frame of mind when, after the collapse of Israel's kingdom, they pointed to the request for a king as the beginning of her downfall in politics and fidelity to Yahweh.

First Samuel introduces Samuel as a hero of Israel who plays the roles of charismatic judge, priest, prophet and

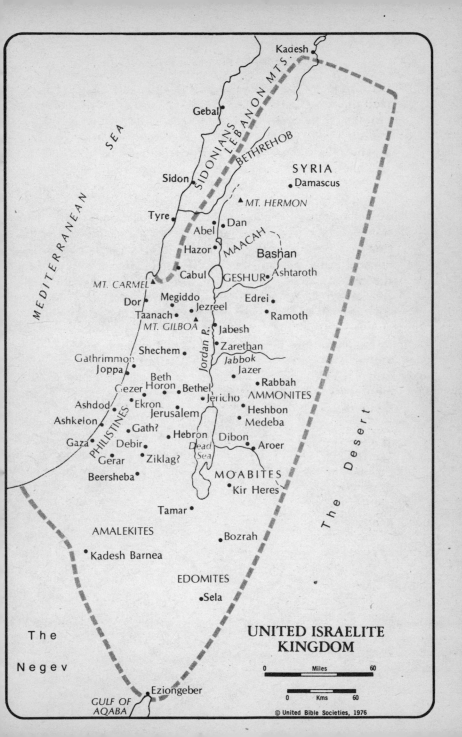

UNITED ISRAELITE
KINGDOM

kingmaker. Many aspects of the miraculous nature of his birth have served as a pattern for New Testament authors concerning Jesus' infancy stories.

During Samuel's days as a judge (circa 1070 B.C.), the Philistine invaders were gaining an upper hand, especially on the southern coast of Canaan. Their monopoly on the production of iron gave them a strategic advantage in battle.

In one skirmish at Aphek, the Israelites carried the Ark of the Covenant into battle for protection, only to have this religious symbol of God's presence captured by the Philistines (First Samuel 4). After a series of defeats, the people turned to Samuel and demanded that he give them a king. We do not know what his personal attitude was toward the monarchy. In one tradition he approves the idea; in the other he selects a king only under great pressure. Samuel did, however, anoint Saul as Israel's first king.

Saul ruled Israel from 1020 to 1000 B.C. As the shaper of the kingship, his career reflects the transition away from the period of the Judges. He is revered as the person who turned the tide of battle against the Philistines, thus giving Israel new hope and a measure of unity.

Saul had no time for the niceties of being a king. During his ruling years most of his days were spent on the battlefield. Archaeologists indicate that his palace at Gibeah was a simple, rustic fortress with no evidence of the trappings of royalty. He shared the simplicity of the people he served as king.

In addition to his victories over the Philistines, Saul was able to subdue the Amalekites and the Gibeonites using a volunteer army. Conscription and military taxation had yet to arrive in Israel. Although Saul never enjoyed the complete support of his people, as David later would, he did serve as a rallying point for the celebration of Israel.

Saul was a brave, yet tragic, figure of Israel's history.

Once David appeared on the scene, Saul's latent fears and jealousy took over. A flaw in his personaltiy led to episodes of manic depression and paranoia described in First Samuel 16:14 as "an evil spirit from the Lord."

To compound Saul's difficulties Samuel withdrew his support and regretted the day he anointed King Saul. In his last days Saul faced odds that would have taxed the capacities of the most balanced personalities.

The open rivalry between Saul and David put a strain on the aging Saul. It is evident that the redactor of First Samuel is pro-David in outlook. He notes that as the popularity of David grew Saul's mental state deteriorated. Saul's irrational fear of his successor forced David to live in a Robin Hood style with the support of his loyal outlaws.

Taking advantage of the conflicts between David and Saul, the Philistines renewed their attacks on the central area of Canaan. On the evening before Saul's army met the Philistines near Gilboa, Saul visited a witch at Endor, seeking through necromancy the advice of the dead Samuel. The word of Samuel foretold the tragic fate that would befall Saul in the morning when the Philistines stormed Mount Gilboa and defeated Saul's army. Among the dead were found the bodies of Saul and his son, Jonathan. Saul's own words seem to be his epitaph: "God has turned away from me and answers me no more" (First Samuel 28:15).

With Saul's defeat at Gilboa, Israel was left at the mercy of the Philistines. As Israel lost ground to her enemies, Saul's son, Ishbaal, tried to gather the remnants of his father's government as a nucleus of another kingdom. His only real support came from the general, Abner, with whom he quarreled constantly. Ishbaal's attempt to succeed his father ended tragically when he was killed by one of his own troops.

The authors of the Old Testament stress that God remained the guiding force in Israel's life. As David was anointed king at Hebron, the stage was set for renewal and an era of greatness was promised. Saul's mental instability forced David to live the life of an outlaw. He gathered around him the discontented and distressed people of Judah, who remained loyal to the new king.

After a seven-year reign at Hebron, David captured a former Jesubite fortress midway between the Northern and Southern Kingdoms and established Jerusalem as the new capital for Israel. After a series of setbacks, his army was victorious over the Philistines and the new king emerged as Israel's hero and savior.

Jerusalem, atop Mount Zion, was a natural fortress. David's choice for his capital reflects his genius. By moving the center of government toward the north, he placated many northerners who had been loyal to Saul's family.

Finally, David brought the Ark of the Covenant to Jerusalem amid great celebration and rejoicing. This act strengthened his ties with the priests and effectively made Jerusalem the center of Israel's cult as well as its government. Second Samuel 7:18–29, which is probably a midrash on these events, tells us that David desired to build a temple for the Lord but was persuaded by the prophet Nathan not to embark on the project. The text contains God's promise that in David an everlasting dynasty will be established. Here we encounter a theme which will develop later in the Old Testament as messianic prophecy.

David's military prowess made him the ruler of the area between Egypt and the Euphrates River. His success in becoming the most powerful ruler of his day was due in part to the fact that there was no other formidable power in the world of the 10th century B.C. Nevertheless, David's military accomplishments were a source of pride and hope for the Israelites.

Second Samuel 11:1–12:25 portrays the brave human character and strength of David's personality. His adultery with Bathsheba and his responsibility for the death of her husband, Uriah, are judged to be the beginning of David's decline. After he was rebuked by Nathan, David publicly acknowledged his sin and asked the Lord's forgiveness. Like many great persons, his true strength was manifest after a moment of weakness.

David's final years as king were marked by intrigue and violence in his court family. Realizing that their father's days were numbered, his sons plotted against David. The ill-fated rebellion of Absalom crushed David's spirit. His lament over his dead son is truly one of the most beautiful passages in Scripture (Second Samuel 18:33).

After an abortive attempt by Adonijah, another of David's sons, to seize the kingship, Solomon was appointed king by his dying father at the request of Bathsheba and Nathan. The reign of King Solomon (961–922 B.C.) signaled another turn in Israel's history. Now the kingship was based on heredity and not on charismatic gifts. Solomon's reign began with signs of unlimited success and ended with his subjects on the verge of rebellion and civil war.

After becoming the king, Solomon began to consolidate David's conquests in order to make Israel one of the great nations of the world. His skills as an organizer enabled him to exercise greater authority over his people. By a series of marriages with the daughters of foreign rulers, Solomon managed to remain at peace with his political rivals. His military establishment was unchallenged and his conscripted army made Israel feared by other nations.

Taking advantage of Israel's strategic position, Solomon established himself as a man of commerce. He used Phoenician sailors and shipbuilders to construct a port at Ezion-geber on the Gulf of Aqaba. Even the Queen of Sheba was impressed by the magnificence of Israel's wealth as a trading power. Solomon exercised an effective monopoly on the horse and chariot business while he controlled the mining of copper. Certainly his was a diversified economy.

Solomon probably is most remembered as a patron of the arts. During his reign culture and learning flourished in Israel. The authors of Scripture speak of Solomon as the patron of the Wisdom Literature. The Temple at Jerusalem was a testimony to his interest in culture. Because he incorporated so many pagan elements in his temple, one wonders if it was more a monument to the King than a temple for the Lord.

When Solomon died after a forty-year reign, many of his "accomplishments" were a mere façade. The people were bitter and close to revolt. Israel was financially exhausted by excessive taxes. The gulf between the rich and the poor was growing ever wider. Poor people lived in hovels in Jerusalem, while Solomon's horses dwelt in stables of ivory. Solomon's many wives brought their paganism to the court. Israel's faithful recognized that Mosaic religion was being tarnished.

A HOUSE DIVIDED
(I KINGS 11–15; 20–22)

By worldly standards, Solomon brought Israel to the zenith of her influence in the political arena. But when he died after forty years as king many of his achievements proved to be hollow. His subjects were bitter and on the verge of revolt. The nation was bankrupt and the poor no longer could bear the burden of excessive taxes. Between the rich and poor a gulf developed that contradicted the Mosaic covenant's idea of community. Solomon's many wives brought paganism to the court, thereby adulterating the religion of Israel. The author of the Deuteronomy 17:14–20 seems to be judging Solomon's reign as a "return to Egypt."

Rehoboam, Solomon's son, succeeded his father. Immediately after being anointed king, he became aware of discontent in the northern areas of his land. He made his way north to Shechem, where Joshua had renewed the covenant after the Hebrews conquered Canaan. He intended to receive a promise of fidelity from the people of the north. In First Kings 12 we read that Rehoboam was confronted with the demand that he lessen the severe policy of his father. Ignoring the advice of the elders, he stubbornly refused to listen to the complaints of the citizens.

One of Solomon's directors of public works, named Jeroboam, was skillful in recognizing the signs of discontent. Playing upon the North's complaints, he organized a government to rival Rehoboam's. The northern kingdom kept the name Israel, while the South became known as Judah, retaining its traditional capital in Jerusalem.

David's kingdom was a divided household. The empire gradually eroded and both states became second-rate powers on the verge of economic collapse.

Rehoboam realized that he could not regain the North. He was faced with disloyalty in his own court and had to devote his entire attention to securing the government in Judah.

The southern kingdom continued to be intimidated by other world powers until 587 B.C., when it was conquered by the Babylonian army. Babylon left Jerusalem in ruins. Its magnificent temple was destroyed and its chief citizens were deported to a foreign land.

When an independent northern state emerged, the people found themselves cut off from Jerusalem and its temple. Shrines were set up in Israel to substitute for the Temple

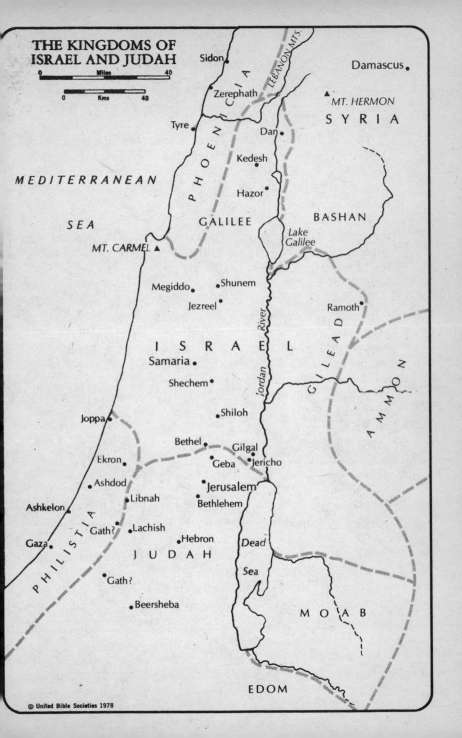

THE KINGDOMS OF ISRAEL AND JUDAH

Miles
0 _____ 40

Kms
0 _____ 40

MEDITERRANEAN

SEA

MT. CARMEL ▲

PHOENICIA

Sidon

Zerephath

Tyre

Dan

Kedesh

Hazor

GALILEE

Lake
Galilee

LEBANON MTS.

Damascus

MT. HERMON ▲

SYRIA

BASHAN

Megiddo

Shunem

Jezreel

Ramoth

ISRAEL

Samaria

Shechem

Shiloh

Bethel

Gilgal

Geba

Jericho

Joppa

Ekron

Ashdod

Jerusalem

Bethlehem

Ashkelon

Libnah

Gath?

Lachish

Gaza

Hebron

JUDAH

Gath?

Beersheba

PHILISTIA

Dead

Sea

Jordan River

GILEAD

AMMON

MOAB

EDOM

© United Bible Societies 1978

of Solomon. One was located at Bethel, near the border of Judah; another was built at Dan, on the northern frontier of Israel.

At the beginning, these shrines reflected orthodox Hebrew faith. As time went on, however, the creation of an independent priesthood and the lack of contact with Jerusalem found them infected by pagan elements. Later, Jeroboam's shrines would be attacked as the epitome of infidelity to Mosaic religion.

When Jeroboam died, there followed a period of civil turmoil which lasted until 876 B.C., when a general, Omri, seized power and founded a new dynasty in Israel. He moved his capital from Shechem to Samaria, near Mount Gerizim. History indicates that he made a significant contribution to the stabilization of Israel. The powerful kingdom of Assyria referred to Israel in official documents as "the house of Omri" while the Bible dismissed his reign in six verses.

An era of peace came to Israel because the world powers, which might have overrun the small nation, were preoccupied with internal problems. Omri's son, Ahab, ruled from 869 to 850 B.C. He is credited with the completion of the building of Samaria. Like Solomon, he conscripted the poor to work on his building projects.

Ahab is best remembered for his marriage to the King of Tyre's daughter, Jezebel. A strong-minded and zealous queen, she set about making the worship of Baal normative at the court of Israel.

After a period of harassment by Jezebel, Elijah the prophet was instrumental in halting the advance of Baalism. Yet the worship of the Canaanite gods remained a temptation for years to come.

After Ahab's death, popular opinion turned against Jezebel. During the revolution that brought King Jehu to power (842 B.C.) and saw the wholesale slaughter of devotees of the Canaanite gods, she was thrown from a window to her death. Her corpse remained unburied in the streets and was eaten by dogs.

Unfortunately, the majority of the Northern Kingdom's rulers repeated the mistakes of Solomon. Until 722 B.C., when Israel was subjugated by Assyria, separate and unequal societies developed in the nation. The poor found themselves at the mercy of the rich.

When the prophets appeared on the scene, they spoke in this corrupt situation, first to Israel and then to Judah. It was the work of the prophet to remind the people that the exploitation of persons did not square with the Mosaic covenant. The stage was set for the voice of prophecy.

V. The Prophets,
Israel's Conscience

PROPHECY IN ISRAEL

Throughout the history of salvation, certain people seem to have been specially chosen by God as his spokesmen. Moses towers above his contemporaries as one who is attuned to God's working among his people. In a similar manner, the tenth century B.C. witnessed the emergence of a unique group of men, the prophets, who claimed to be speaking as divine messengers. Prophecy thrived until the fourth century B.C. While a variety of men were called to be prophets, one attribute was shared by all: Each had been elected by God to address his word to Israel.

Many people define a prophet as "one who predicts." Foretelling the future is not, however, essential for prophecy. To be a prophet one need not spend time peering into a crystal ball. According to the Old Testament, the main concern of the prophet was to address God's word to the present. The prophets sometimes spoke about the future, but not in the capacity of soothsayers. Rather, they saw tragic implications for Israel's future in the choices the people were making against their God. In an attempt to remedy the present, the prophets often spoke warnings about the future.

Conservative by nature, these zealous ambassadors bid the people of God return to authentic Mosaic religion. There are elements that may strike the modern reader as unusual or even bizarre in the prophetic literature. Prophecy in Israel was affected by the same phenomenon among her neighbors. Yet, the prime concern of biblical prophecy was a religious and moral one.

We cannot separate the prophets from the times in which they preached. To adequately understand their message, one must be familiar with the historical events of their day. These men did not stand apart from society; nor did they speak in a political or cultural vacuum. They were intensely involved in the problems of their day, sharing all aspects of life with the people to whom they ministered. The prophet was not a loner who had removed himself from the mainstream of life. Each prophet spoke in a definite historical situation. To ignore the context of prophecy is to misinterpret a large portion of biblical literature.

Whenever a prophet appeared on the scene, he claimed to have been appointed by God to deliver a message to Israel. Often the words of the prophet upset a complacent people. He prodded the collective conscience of God's people by reminding them that fidelity to the Mosaic covenant was chiefly determined by interior dispositions rather than by formalistic religious observance.

At a time when influential Israelites forgot or ignored the social dimension of the covenant, these brave individuals confronted their contemporaries with the reality of sin and injustice. Popularity, especially popularity with the "establishment," was seldom a hallmark of prophetism. Frequently, the prophets found themselves persecuted because their words ran counter to so many of the vested interests of their day.

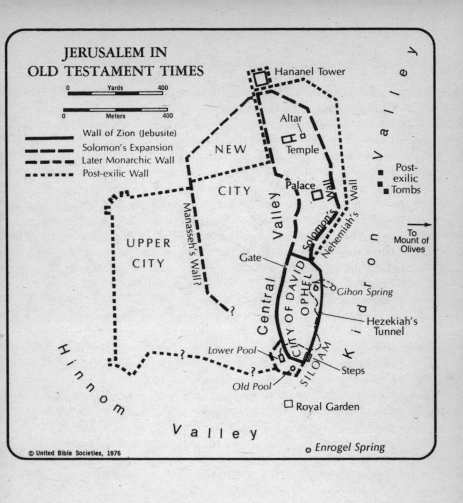

JERUSALEM IN OLD TESTAMENT TIMES

Wall of Zion (Jebusite)
Solomon's Expansion
Later Monarchic Wall
Post-exilic Wall

Hananel Tower

NEW CITY

Altar
Temple

Palace

Solomon's Wall

Nehemiah's Wall

Post-exilic Tombs

To Mount of Olives

Manasseh's Wall?

UPPER CITY

Gate

Central Valley

CITY OF DAVID

OPHEL

Gihon Spring

Hezekiah's Tunnel

Lower Pool

SILOAM

Steps

Old Pool

Royal Garden

Kidron Valley

Hinnom Valley

Enrogel Spring

© United Bible Societies, 1976

The religious dimension of politics was a subject of their concern. As paganism slowly infected the structures of Israel's government, the prophets spoke out against the adulteration of Mosaic faith. They advised kings and princes to trust in God rather than in political intrigue and alliances. The king could usually depend on the prophet's not telling him what he wanted to hear. Servile flattery was foreign to the prophetic style.

Caught up by the dynamic power of God's word, the prophet frequently pointed to the abusive dangers in organized religion. When many lived with the attitude that the correct performance of ritual was the chief element of religion, the prophets called attention to the fact that faith was a matter of the heart. The prophets told the priests of Israel that God despised their sacrifices because the needs of the poor were being ignored while ritual was executed with meticulous precision.

Idolatry was a constant temptation. Not only did the prophets reject the worship of foreign gods, they also warned of the paganistic tendency of super-patriotism and exclusive nationalism. Time and again they told Israel that God had elected her not to a position of privilege but to share the responsibility of mediating God's word to all people. To confront the possibility that God might love the enemies of Israel was unsettling to say the least.

What relevance do these "troublers of Israel" have for us today? The answer can be found all about us. Like ancient Israel, we run the risk of religious formalism. We have new forms of idolatry and paganism. We live in a society that puts great value on possessions and devalues persons. The words of the prophets, such as Amos, Isaiah and Jeremiah, are still relevant because, unfortunately, we have yet to take them with the seriousness they deserve.

ELIJAH, A LONELY VOICE FOR FAITH (I KINGS 17–19, II KINGS 1–2)

Long before the prophets whose messages survive as books of the Old Testament were active in Israel, two giants in prophetic tradition spoke God's Word in the Northern Kingdom. The stories about Elijah and Elisha, found in the books of Kings, are testimony to popular admiration for them.

The career of Elijah must be understood against the backdrop of King Ahab's rule in Israel (869–850 B.C.). Ahab had married Jezebel, the daughter of Ethbaal, who was the pagan king of Tyre. When this strong-minded woman arrived in Israel, she was not satisfied to worship her gods in private. Instead, she attempted to impose Baalism upon her subjects. When she erected a temple to honor Baal and initiated a persecution of the Yahwistic prophets, syncretistic dangers to Mosaic religion became blatantly evident.

Elijah's zealous fidelity to the God of Israel is attested by the Hebrew meaning of his name, "Yahweh is my God." His life was spent in direct confrontation with the pagan worship of Queen Jezebel. Long after his ministry ended, his devoted disciples circulated legends about him so that his fame grew beyond the scope of the human. Finally, Elijah achieved such a heroic status in Israel's faith that tradition said he would herald the dawn of the end of time, the eschatological age.

Elijah steps onto the biblical stage as he mysteriously arrives from Tishbe in Gilead to inform King Ahab of an imminent drought. In the midst of the famine that followed, Elijah accomplished great miracles which became favorites of popular legend. Uppermost was the prophet's concern to stress the sovereignty of the Lord over nature and in the lives of his people.

King Ahab viewed Elijah as the "troubler of Israel." No doubt he had in mind the great disturbance the prophet had caused by his news of the drought and famine. Elijah accused Ahab of being the real troublemaker because of his tolerance of Baal worship in Israel.

One of the most dramatic scenes in the Bible occurs in First Kings 18, when Elijah challenges the devotees of Baal to a contest on Mount Carmel. Elijah stands as the lone prophet of the Lord in direct confrontation with 450 prophets of Baal. As two altars of sacrifice were erected, the prophets of Baal were invited to petition their gods to ignite the holocaust on their altar. They danced around the altar uttering frenzied incantations as they slashed their flesh with swords. But no answer came from the Baals.

Then Elijah moved forward and, with a touch of humor, ridiculed the silence of the Baals. He ordered water to be poured over his altar three times. Then, with a simple prayer, he asked the God of Israel to bring fire upon the altar. Elijah's faith was vindicated as the sacrifice burned violently. After the prophets of Baal were murdered, rain fell upon Israel, soaking the parched land.

Actually, Elijah's victory was incomplete. Jezebel, still the dominant force at Israel's court, resolved to silence his disturbing voice. The prophet fled south into the territory of Judah. The Lord supported and strengthened him as he journeyed as far as Horeb or Sinai, the scene of the beginnings of Mosaic faith.

With the revelation to Moses as a model, the biblical author describes Elijah's renewal at the source of Israel's faith. The traditional imagery of the theophany is reversed. The Lord does not speak from the earthquake, fire or wind. Now his voice comes to Elijah in a "gentle stillness." Elijah's experience at Horeb is important because it indicates that the prophets are not radical innovators but, rather, spokesmen who demand a return to the authentic covenant religion of Mosaic times.

In First Kings 21, Elijah meets Ahab again. This time the issue is the King's confiscation of Naboth's vineyard. At the urging of Jezebel, Ahab had Naboth and his sons murdered so that he could take over his land for a country estate. Elijah's confrontation of the King on this issue serves as a preface to the social message of the prophets of a later age.

The Black spiritual "Swing Low Sweet Chariot" exemplifies the popular legend that Elijah departed in a whirlwind and a chariot of fire. Tradition built on this theme to say that Elijah would return again as the precursor of the Messianic Age. In the New Testament, both Jesus and John the Baptist were mistaken for the returning Elijah.

Elijah stands as a dour and lonely figure who is a stubborn champion of orthodoxy against seemingly overwhelming odds. His persistent strength was not his alone. The Lord's fidelity to Elijah encourages the person of faith in any age.

THE EIGHTH CENTURY PROPHETS

Amos, First of the Writing Prophets

With the career of Amos of Tekoa, a new period in the development of prophetic office began in Israel. His book represents the first time prophetic oracles were preserved in a separate biblical book. Amos is commonly called the first of the writing prophets. This does not imply that Amos himself was responsible for the book in its written form. The actual compilation was the work of his devoted disciples who believed that the oracles of their teacher were worth passing on to future generations.

The Book of Amos provides a measure of biographical information about the prophet. His ministry occurred during the reign of King Jeroboam II (786–746 B.C.). It was a time of prosperity in Israel. However, the wealth of the people fostered greed and social injustice. Amos was called to be a prophet in the midst of a growing conflict between the rich and the poor. His home was in the village of Tekoa, about ten miles south of Jerusalem. Tekoa may have been a Judean military fortress and, because such a wide variety of people would pass through it, Amos may have been aware of the corruption that existed in the northern kingdom.

As a layman Amos seems to have had a dual occupation. In addition to being a shepherd he was a dresser of sycamore trees. The fruit of the sycamore was the diet of the poor. While unripe, it had to be punctured to help it ripen to an edible state. This work gave Amos a direct contact with the plight of the poor.

When he assumed his prophetic office, Amos left his native Judah and went to the centers of corruption in Israel, there to deliver the word of God to a society that had drifted far from Mosaic ideals.

Economic prosperity had resulted in social upheaval. The peasants and farmers, who had been the backbone of the nation, now found themselves oppressed by the avaricious nobility. Poor people were dispossessed as their small plots of land were taken to form new country estates. Because judges decided cases based on the bribes given by the noble rich no appeal could be made at court.

In the midst of this adulteration of the Mosaic covenant, religious devotion and cult flourished. The sanctuary at Bethel was filled to overflowing with worshippers offering expensive gifts and sacrifices. A formalism in ritual characterized the religion of Israel. Few people seemed to care that the dehumanizing lot of the poor was a direct conflict with the faith they professed.

Into this corrupt situation, which valued possessions over people, Amos came preaching a message of social justice based on covenant faith. At a time when the professional prophets were conspicuous by their silence, religious functionaries seemed blind to the critical nature of the times and the rich closed their eyes to the poor in their streets, Amos was taken from his flock and sent as the Lord's prophet to Israel.

The Book of Amos begins with a series of oracles against the neighbors of Israel. We can picture the smug complacency of his listeners as they heard their enemies excoriated. But imagine their surprise when the subject of his final indictment was Israel herself! With fury, Amos denounced his own people for their multiple sins of injustice. The book ends with a series of visions concerning the impending doom of Israel. The "Day of the Lord" had been anticipated as a time when the Lord would secure victory for Israel over her foes. Now, Amos viewed this "Day" as a time of judgment and wrath because Israel had forgotten the social implications of Mosaic faith.

It was Amos's firm contention that Israel had been chosen by God to have a special responsibility to the peoples of the world. The message of Amos is a universal one. It views Israel's vocation as one of service, not privilege. He decried the irresponsibility of the rich in forming a social pyramid. Class distinction was denying the brotherhood of the covenant and was bringing doom upon the People of God.

When Amos met the religious hypocrisy of the day head-on, the priest Amaziah denounced him to Jeroboam as a conspirator against the government. Like any true prophet, Amos disturbed the complacent religious fraud who divorced piety from life. Amaziah reflects the attitude we so often take when confronted with inconsistency in our religious lifestyle: "O seer, go flee away" (Amos 7:12).

What is the relevance of Amos for a believer in the last quarter of the twentieth century? The answer is as obvious as the many examples of social injustice that confront the contemporary believer. The person of faith will still be awed by God's word spoken through Amos: "I hate, I despise your feasts, and I take no delight in your solemn assemblies. . . . Take away from me the noise of your songs. . . . But let justice roll down like waters, and righteousness like an ever-flowing stream" (Amos 6:21–24).

Hosea, Prophet of Divine Love

In the twilight years of the northern kingdom, the prophet Hosea addressed himself to the people of Israel, delivering an eloquent reminder that God's love for his chosen ones had no limits. Hosea was a younger contemporary of Amos. Most authors place his ministry between 745 and 725 B.C., during the final years of King Jeroboam II's reign. This was the turbulent period immediately preceding Samaria's humiliation by Assyria.

Hosea has the distinction of being the only writing prophet to be a native of Israel and to have had his ministry there. Very few biographical details exist. He seems, however, to have been more cosmopolitan than Amos. The illustrations he used reflect a deep sensitivity for the plight of the common people.

The prophet's words were delivered orally before they were written. Because the book reflects a cross section of Hosea's preaching, it is difficult to read. Textually, it might be termed corrupt. It has been poorly preserved through the centuries and, hence, there are many variant readings and the meanings of words are not always clear.

Both Amos and Hosea based their messages on the same theology. They stressed fidelity to God as outlined in the Mosaic covenant. Each gave prominent place to the social responsibilities of the People of God.

Whereas Amos projects the personality of a stern and austere shepherd, Hosea personifies the loving kindness that he preached. Hosea was a poet who was deeply in love with the people he felt obliged to condemn. Like a loving father, he experienced the conflicting emotions of one who must punish an erring child.

In the first section of the book, we read the account of Hosea's tragic marriage to the unfaithful Gomer. Chapters 1–3 are confusing because the precise order of events is unclear. On one hand, it seems as if Gomer's infidelity began after their marriage; on the other, we are given the impression that Hosea, heeding the command of the Lord, married a prostitute.

Of one thing we are certain: Hosea was committed to his wife. Her repeated adultery did not diminish his love for her. Time and again, the prophet offered her generous forgiveness and the opportunity to begin anew. Hosea's life with Gomer gave him a keen sense of God's unbounded love for Israel. He could not help but contrast that love with the constant infidelity of Israel.

Sacred prostitution was a common religious practice in Canaan. In using the marriage imagery, Hosea ran the risk of degrading the love of God for Israel. He knew that his listeners might assume that the Lord was the husband of Israel in the same manner as Baal was the husband of the land. This might result in Israel's adopting some of the fertility rites of the Canaänites.

Although his allegory was daring, it did serve to remind Israel of God's fidelity and love for her. We must remember that the prophet's starting point was the love of God for Israel not Hosea's love for Gomer. In the language of the artist: God's love was the original and Hosea's was the copy. Saint Paul used a similar parallel when he spoke of the love of Christ for the Church as the pattern for Christian married life.

Hosea encountered the same social evils as Amos. Insightfully, he noted that Israel by its injustice had repudiated its covenant-relationship with the Lord. Trusting in the Baals, military force and several foreign alliances, she had forsaken her Father. This, for Hosea, was the root of sin: for Israel to rely on anyone or anything in place of God.

God's judgment on Israel's sinfulness and infidelity was not an arbitrary action; rather, Israel's collapse was a consequence of sin itself. Israel, by her infidelity might bring herself to the verge of slavery and annihilation, but God would not abandon his people.

Hosea entreated Israel to return to a knowledge of God. By knowledge he meant not factual information but personal knowledge acquired through the shared experience of trust and love. In Hosea's mind, God required not formal acknowledgment so as much as a total commitment.

Reminding Israel that covenant love was rooted in the Exodus experience, the prophet called upon his people to return to the Lord. Because his ways are not man's ways, the Lord would heal the sickness of Israel by his free, unmerited and boundless love.

Hosea's story of Israel's sin and God's loving kindness is more than a historical vignette. Israel's infidelity mirrors our own. The preaching of Hosea comes alive for all who experience the reality of sin as contrasted with the loving forgiveness of the Father. Hosea's words flood God's People with the joyous good news that our sins are pardoned.

At the same time, they remind us that the person who had received God's loving kindness has the responsibility of sharing his or her gift. "For I desire steadfast love and not sacrifice, the knowledge of God, rather than burnt offerings" (Hosea 6:6).

Micah, Champion of the Poor

At the close of the eighth century B.C., the village of Moresheth, in the foothills of southwestern Palestine, was singularly unimpressive. It was little more than a stopover for traders and soldiers passing through Judah. From this humble locale came Micah, a prophet who reflected the spirit of Amos, Hosea and Isaiah.

Micah had a special predilection for the poor farmers and shepherds of his country. In his judgment, it was these uncomplicated people who were the mainstay of the nation. The exploitation of the Judean peasants indicated to Micah that the crimes of Israel's rich and powerful ruling class had overflowed into his beloved Judah.

For a half-century, Israel had enjoyed a period of economic growth and stable peace. King Jeroboam II's reign was marked by extreme wealth and poverty. When he died, the Northern Kingdom found itself threatened by the might of Assyria. Damascus had fallen to Assyrian troops in 731 B.C. The question being asked in Micah's days was: With Syria in ruins, could a similar fate be awaiting Israel?

When Micah was young, Amos was active in proclaiming his message of social justice. It seems that Micah was familiar with Amos's words. The greatness of both prophets shines out in their fierce defense of the rights of an oppressed poor. Many of the rebukes Amos delivered against the corruption in Israel during Jeroboam II's reign are restated by Micah. His primary focus is Judah during the reigns of Jotham (750–735 B.C.), Ahaz (735–715 B.C.) and Hezekiah (715–687 B.C.).

The book begins in the form of a covenant lawsuit in which the Lord comes from his heavenly temple atop the mountains to judge Samaria and Jerusalem. These capital cities had become centers of moral corruption and crass materialism. By their hatred of good and love for evil, their leaders had prostituted Mosaic faith.

Micah spoke to a Samaria under attack from Assyria. Knowing that Israel could not possibly withstand the attack, he tried to awaken its capitol to the reality of imminent destruction. To Jerusalem, Micah indicated that its citizens should learn a lesson from Israel's collapse. Using symbolic language to speak of the corrupting influence of the fertility cults, he suggested that the sins of the north were spilling over into Judah. He pronounced his judgment upon prophets, rulers, priests and judges. Because of their wickedness, Micah attested that Jerusalem would one day be a heap of ruins.

Micah was caustic in his criticism of the professional prophets whose oracles depended upon what those who paid them wished to hear. The superficiality of the official prophets prompted Micah himself to assume their office of proclaiming God's judgment upon his people.

At Jerusalem Micah pointed to the criminal profiteering of civil officials. Judges were taking bribes and priests were managing oracles to fill their coffers. His rural background made him aware of the sense of responsibility that should characterize political and religious leaders. No amount of confidence in external liturgy was capable of saving a people who permitted oppression, bribery, injustice and corruption to flourish in its cities.

Micah does not deserve the title "prophet of doom." On the contrary, he holds out the hope that the fidelity of Israel to her God will shine out in the lives of a remnant people. It was Micah's strong conviction that, through this remnant, God's covenant-promises would continue the history of salvation.

Like Hosea, Micah looked at the infidelity of his people and promised that God would sustain them in spite of their sin. But, as with a parent who must chastise an erring child, Micah said, the punishment of the Lord would be tempered with steadfast love.

The Book of Micah contains one of the best summaries of the spirit of authentic religion found in the Bible: "What does the Lord require of you but to do justice, and to love kindness, and to walk humbly with your God?" (Micah 6:8). With this he captures the essence of prophetic religion as exemplified by Amos (justice), Hosea (love, kindness) and Isaiah (humility before God). Not only Judah but every person of faith is provided with a simple test for religious devotion: Am I just in all my dealings? Am I kind to all people? Am I living in humble community with God?

Isaiah, Man of Faith (Isaiah 1–39)

When a person reads the Book of Isaiah, he or she is aware that modern concepts of authorship did not prevail in ancient Israel. Its core is from the prophet Isaiah, but much of the material is the product of the prophet's disciples and interpreters who lived many generations later.

Most contemporary scholars agree that chapters 40–66 were not written in the eighth century B.C., when Isaiah's career was in progress. These chapters reflect the situation almost two centuries later, after Judah had fallen to Babylon. Their contents apply the message of Isaiah to new circumstances of life. Our reflections here are confined to the material found in chapters 1–39.

One of Israel's most gifted poets, Isaiah was a person of deep religious thought. He was born in Jerusalem about 760 B.C. and his ministry as prophet was at a critical juncture in Israel's history. The Northern Kingdom was in a period of decline and it was only a matter of years before it would fall to the mighty army of Assyria (721 B.C.).

In Judah, an era of stability under King Uzziah had ended. King Ahaz seems to have been a weak and ineffectual leader in Jerusalem. Ahaz made an alliance with Tiglath-pileser of Assyria, so that when Israel was conquered Judah was spared and made a vassal state of Assyria. Ahaz apparently was willing to surrender his people's faith for the religion of Assyria and went to the extreme of erecting a pagan altar in the Jerusalem Temple. As all sorts of foreign practices and superstitions began to bring social and moral decay to Jerusalem, Isaiah could not be silent.

Isaiah opposed Ahaz's plan to seek protection from Assyria. He viewed foreign alliances as compromising the religious and political freedom of Judah. Faith in God, he maintained, was the key to Judah's survival.

After Ahaz made his treaty with Assyria, Isaiah withdrew from public life. He may have spent the years 734–715 B.C. with his disciples. It seems that he made no public statements during these years. When Hezekiah became king in 715 B.C., Isaiah tried to keep him from taking part in the Egyptian plots against Assyria. Isaiah viewed Assyria as the ruthless instrument of God's judgment upon Judah.

When Sargon II of Assyria died in 705 B.C., there was a general revolt against his oppressive nation. As Hezekiah was drawn into an alliance against Assyria, Isaiah said that he had made a "covenant with death." Although Assyria did not conquer Jerusalem, Judah was decisively under its sway. Politically and religiously Isaiah's policy of nonalliance seems to have been the correct path to follow.

Isaiah's faith was a tower of strength in the tumultuous years of crisis. In the midst of civil and international chaos, he relied on the certainty that God determines the course of history. He viewed the Assyrians as the rod of God's anger. If, however, Assyria overstepped its bounds, God would destroy its power by his sovereignty.

Isaiah was called to be a prophet in a Temple vision recorded in chapter 6. Face to face with the transcendent holiness of God, he became conscious of his own unworthiness as a "man of unclean lips." The symbolic cleansing by the burning coal prepared him for his ministry of service.

The glory of God's holiness was expressed in his judgment upon human sin. Sin, by its very nature, is uncleanness and rebellion against the Lord. Like Amos, Isaiah saw the whole society tainted by a sin for which sacrifice was a useless remedy. He proclaimed a Day of God's Judgment that would extend to all people. To counter men's pride and arrogance, Isaiah proposed faith in God, rather than man, as the remedy for sin.

Although the days ahead seemed bleak for Judah, Isaiah looked to the future and spoke of a "remnant" that would survive the period of judgment to be the vehicle of continuing salvation history. Centuries later, this "remnant" would return from a generation of exile as a purified Israel with a mission of being a light of salvation to all nations.

During the Christmas season when Christians focus upon Jesus as the promised Messiah of Israel, many of the Gospel concepts used to explain him have their roots in the prophecy of Isaiah. In the eighth century B.C., he expressed dissatisfaction with earthly rulers by looking with hopeful expectation to a future "anointed one from God." With serene confidence, he projected into the future a society where justice and peace would be a way of life and in which an ideal Davidic king would reign forever.

The themes and words of Isaiah provided an apt manner of expression when the early Christian community tried to come to terms with the significance and meaning of Jesus. Isaiah's uncompromised hope came to life seven centuries later when an announcement was made to Mary: "You will become pregnant and give birth to a son, and you will name him Jesus. . . . The Lord God will make him a king, as his ancestor David was . . . and his kingdom will never end!" (Luke 1:31–33).

THE SEVENTH AND SIXTH CENTURY PROPHETS

Zephaniah, Mediator of God's Judgment

After Isaiah, the voice of prophecy was relatively silent for seventy-five years until Zephaniah emerged as a spokes-man for the Lord in the mid-seventh century B.C. His message confirms that the influence of prophetic faith survived during a dark age of infidelity following the days of Isaiah. Zephaniah reinterpreted the words of Amos and Isaiah and spoke forcefully concerning God's judgment on the sins of Judah.

During the years prior to Zephaniah's career, Judah found herself under the complete control of Assyria. In the early seventh century B.C., Assyria extended her influence westward. Assyrian armies invaded Egypt, captured the Pharaoh and stretched Assyrian domination as far south as Memphis. In 661 B.C., Ashurbanipal subjugated Thebes, the capital of Egypt, and Assyria reached the high point of her world conquests.

The king of Judah in this period of conquest was Manasseh (687–642 B.C.). His rule was remembered for its cruelty and wickedness. Although he had to pay political tribute to Assyria, his real sin was his religious apostasy. He actively supported the adoption of Assyrian cult and customs in Judah, thus undoing the reform of Hezekiah, his father.

Second Kings 21:1–18 recounts that Manasseh introduced the Assyrian practice of worshipping the stars by erecting altars for the astral deities in the Jerusalem Temple: "He burned his son as an offering, and practiced soothsaying and augury, and dealt with mediums and with wizards" (Second Kings 21:6). In these terrible days, those who dared to oppose the king paid with their lives.

Manasseh's son was like his father. Amon ruled for two years before he was assassinated. The new king, Josiah, came to the throne at the age of eight. When this child-king became an adult he instituted a thorough reformation of Judaean religion.

Zephaniah's prophetic ministry probably began sometime in those early years of Josiah's reign (640–626 B.C.). At this time Scythian invaders from the steppes of southern Russia were sweeping through Egypt and Phoenicia. Their raids signaled the downfall of the mighty Assyrian empire. Zephaniah viewed these invasions as a harbinger of God's judgment upon Judah and her neighbors. He denounced the skepticism, idolatry and immorality that were characteristic of the reigns of Manasseh and Amon.

There are four major sections of his book: (1) the significance of the Day of the Lord (1:1–2:3); (2) an indictment of the pagan nations (2:4–15); (3) prophecy against Jerusalem (3:1–8) and (4) promises of home for the future (3:9–20).

Virtually nothing is known about Zephaniah himself. The editor of the book endeavors to show his continuity with the reform of King Hezekiah by naming the king as the prophet's grandfather. Like Amos, Zephaniah was a stern and austere prophet of the justice and judgment of God.

Courageously, Zephaniah pointed to the religious sin of his people. He described the Lord searching Jerusalem with a lamp that exposed the corruption of the proud city. Its people were rebellious and deaf to the Lord's word. The strong were devouring the weak.

Zephaniah, like Amos, awaited the Day of the Lord as a time when God's wrath would be visited on Judah. The leading classes of Jerusalem were condemned for cultic and ethical abuses. Religious functionaries had become corrupt. "Her prophets are wanton, faithless men; her priests profane what is sacred, they do violence to the law" (3:3).

Zephaniah indicates that the divided allegiance of God's people is abhorrent. To worship God and Baal or to confess faith in the Lord and burn incense to the astral deities on the rooftops are actions that, the prophet stressed, indicate Judah's total rejection of her Lord.

Here the message of Zephaniah has a timeless quality. People of faith always have been tempted to give priority to someone or something other than God. Whether the idol be power, success, money, ambition, the family or one's nation, the warning of Jesus echoes the theme of Zephaniah: "No one can serve two masters" (Matthew 6:24).

With Isaiah, Zephaniah indicates that the Day of the Lord will be a period of refinement and purification which will root out the practical atheism of an indifferent people. To counter the capital sin of pride, Zephaniah counsels a quiet, trustful humility before God.

At the conclusion of the book, Zephaniah held out a great hope for the remnant of the People of God. The future glory of Israel will arrive when the Lord renews his people in his steadfast love. The prophet sees the Lord as the ultimate vindicator of his people.

Zephaniah's oracle concludes with these words: "I will rescue all the lame and bring the exiles home. I will turn their shame into honor, and all the world will praise them. I will bring your scattered people home; I will make you famous throughout the world and make you prosperous once again" (Zephaniah 3:19–20).

Nahum and Habakkuk, Prophets of Nationalism

Nahum. Assyrian reluctance to record their military failures explains why no testimony to the empire's decline remains. Neo-Babylonian annals tell us that in 625 B.C. Nabopolesser founded a Babylonian state and, after securing control of Babylon, moved in the direction of Assyria. In 612 B.C., the Babylonian king destroyed Nineveh. Its collapse marked the end of an epoch in world history. This event is the focus of Nahum's oracle.

For more than two centuries both Judah and Israel had been oppressed by the Assyrians. The armies of Assyria had been responsible for the downfall of the Northern Kingdom and had effectively reduced Judah to a vassal status. Without a doubt, great rejoicing in the streets of Jerusalem greeted the news of Assyria's demise.

The prophet Nahum interpreted the defeat of Assyria as evidence of the triumph of Israel's God over her pagan enemies. Some commentators believe that his original oracles were redacted to compose a liturgy for the Jerusalem Temple in which the humiliation of Assyria was celebrated as one of God's mighty acts on behalf of his people.

The meaning of the prophet's name, "comfort" or "compassion," hardly reveals his attitude toward the Assyrians. We know nothing about this seventh-century prophet other than that he was born in Elkosh, probably a small town in southwestern Judah. A genius in the use of poetic imagery, Nahum was a firm believer in God's all-pervasive power in the world. His poetry evidences his strong nationalistic loyalties to Judah.

Although the book is only a few pages in length, it has a disparate flavor. Chapter 1 contains an alphabetic acrostic hymn praising God's might as shown in nature. Alternating threats and promises are characteristic of these poems.

Nahum's two final chapters contain a vivid description of the fall of Nineveh. The details are so precisely drawn that many authors conjectured that he may have been an eyewitness to the event. However, internal evidence indicates that Nahum's fertile imagination and stinging invective against the Assyrians led him to compose the oracle prior to the defeat of Nineveh. Perhaps his prophecy is a product of wishful thinking.

It is difficult to reconcile the tone of the book with Jesus' admonition that we should forgive and love our enemies. Unlike the other prophets, Nahum's concern is not national corruption or infidelity. Rather, the defeat of a hated oppressor is the occasion for his praise of the Lord's jealous wrath directed against Assyria. Isaiah had said that Assyria would be the Lord's instrument of punishment for Israel and Judah; now Nahum exults that God's judgment is turned against the former "rod of his anger."

From the literary point of view, we can admire the picturesque detail in Nahum's writing. Although the book does not scratch the surface of the forgiveness Christ preached, it does stand as a witness to the prophet's belief that all peoples are subject to God's controlling power and sovereign majesty.

Habakkuk. As the seventh century B.C. ended, the Babylonian empire extended its control over more of the Middle East. While this happened, King Jehoiakim of Judah reversed the reforms of his father, Josiah. Judah again lapsed into apostasy. The prophet Habakkuk viewed the Babylonians or Chaldeans as God's instrument of judgment directed against Judah. Speaking at a crucial juncture in Judah's history, he wrestled with the problem of faith as he saw God's afflicted people about to undergo the humiliation of the Babylonian Exile.

We know nothing personal about this prophet. Habakkuk seems to have been a man of keenly developed moral sense. His literary genius rivals the descriptive sections in the last two chapters of Nahum. From the perspective of faith, Habakkuk questioned God's punishment of Judah, seeing it as inconsistent with the portrait of a loving Father who forgives his people.

Habakkuk was accustomed to climbing a watchtower, where he reflected in isolation upon God's mysterious ways. In chapter 2, he withdraws to his retreat, awaiting the Word of the Lord. Under divine guidance Habakkuk became aware that "Those who are evil will not survive, but those who are righteous will live because they are faithful to God" (Habakkuk 2:4).

The Christian apostle, Paul, used Habakkuk's words to draw a contrast between a justification that depends on the efforts of a person to earn God's grace, and one that is received as an unmerited gift from God (Romans 1:17, 3:21–22; Galatians 3:1:11).

It remains a practical religious problem to explain the apparent success of the person who does evil as against the failure of the righteous. The Book of Habakkuk offers a personal testimony. It is not by one who had solved the dilemma, but that of a prophet whose troubled spirit confronted the long-suffering qualities of God's patience. The person of faith may wish God's punishment on evildoers to be swift and complete; the God in whom we believe continues to offer salvation and mercy to all peoples.

Jeremiah, the Herald of Hope

"I chose you before I gave you life, and before you were born I selected you to be a prophet to the nations" (Jeremiah 1:4). During the final years of Judah's independence, God's call came to a young man, Jeremiah, giving him authority to speak as a prophet. His prophetic activity spans the years 626–580 B.C. By the end of his career, the once magnificent Jerusalem lay in ruins and the People of God were captive exiles in Babylon.

Unlike the case with other prophets, there is much biographical material about Jeremiah in the Bible. He was acquainted with tragedy, but his life was marked by an unquenchable hope. Called to be a prophet in his teen-age years, his first reaction to the divine summons was to point out the inadequacies of his tender years. He did not want to be a prophet; nevertheless, the Lord's word took hold of Jeremiah. His source of strength was his acute awareness of God's presence. He was a sensitive man by nature and his oracles reveal much about him as a person of changing mood and temper.

Jeremiah was born about 650 B.C. at Anathoth, a city three miles northeast of Jerusalem. He was from a family of priests, possibly a descendant of Abithar, the high priest banished to Anathoth by King Solomon. His career as prophet coincided with a crucial time in Judah's history. Trapped between Egypt, Assyria and Babylon, his tiny nation struggled for survival.

Josiah, the reforming king of Judah, was killed at Megiddo in 609 B.C. and Egypt extended more control over Judah. When the Babylonians defeated the Egyptians at Carchemish in 605 B.C., Judah became the vassal state of Babylon. After a series of weak, ineffectual kings, Judah finally began to bow under Babylonian oppression.

The first wave of Judeans were taken to Babylon as

exiles in 597 B.C. By 587 B.C. the deportation of Jerusalem's leading citizens was complete. In this tragic era, Jeremiah addressed the Lord's Word to a people whom he loved passionately. He viewed the fall of Jerusalem not only as a political and military humiliation.

From his perspective it was a spiritual and moral disaster which finally overtook a rebellious people. As he observed the dissolution of his nation, Jeremiah came to see the fidelity of God as operative in a new way. In Judah's darkest hour, he voiced his clear hope for a new day based on covenant faith (Jeremiah 31:31).

It is evident that the contents of the Book of Jeremiah are disjointed and that the sections are not arranged in chronological order. We can discern several stages in its origins. During the reign of King Jehoikim (609–598 B.C.), Baruch, Jeremiah's faithful secretary, wrote a scroll containing Jeremiah's dedicated words. The king was enraged when he read it and, to indicate his contempt, he threw it into the fire. Baruch copied another version of the prophet's oracles which became an expanded edition of Jeremiah's messages and experiences during the first half of his ministry.

The contents of this second scroll are found in Jeremiah 1–20. Chapters 21–52 reflect the words of someone other than the prophet, presumably Baruch's record of Jeremiah's deeds and prophecy. These biographical reflections were composed after the fall of Jerusalem.

Various literary forms make the work of analysis difficult. There are three distinct varieties of literature in the book: poetic sayings, biographical prose and prose discourses. Far more significant is the theological message the various editors and composers of Jeremiah were attempting to mediate to their readers.

Jeremiah was a captive of God's word. As a true prophet, he was aware that people do not control the Word; rather, the prophet must listen and wait in obedience to God's promptings. Knowledge of the Lord was an essential ingredient in Israel's religion. Whenever this knowledge was lacking, Israel failed. Like Hosea, Jeremiah spelled out knowledge of God in terms of a relationship in loving fidelity to the Father. In the time of the "new covenant," he believed that it would no longer be necessary to admonish Israel to "know the Lord," for she would know him through the forgiveness of her sins.

The election of Israel by God is an important theme in Jeremiah. He viewed Israel as the Lord's special possession whose existence depended upon God's gracious goodness. God required of Israel steadfast love and justice. Jeremiah characterized sin as a stubborn refusal to respond to God's love. It was a perversion of Israel's true identity.

As misfortune followed misfortune, Jeremiah interpreted Judah's fall as a consequence of her disobedience and failure to serve the Lord.

In several places Jeremiah seems to attack the cult of Judah. In itself, Jeremiah said, the Temple had no efficacy. Like the shrine at Shiloh, it would be destroyed because its devotees had violated the spirit of true worship (Jeremiah 7:1–15). Sacrifice in itself was not adequate to ward off the imminent destruction of Jerusalem. Like Amos and Isaiah, Jeremiah insisted that the mechanics of prayer and worship had no meaning unless a person's inward spirit was oriented to the Lord.

Although his words confronted the dying Judah with the consequences of her years of infidelity, Jeremiah held out a hope for a brighter future. As Judah was crumbling under the weight of the Babylonian invasions, he purchased a plot of land at Anathoth, a symbolic gesture indicating that there was a future for his people in their Promised Land.

Jeremiah looked to the day when Israel would carry

God's word in her heart. The rejuvenated Israel would be motivated from within (Jeremiah 31:31). At the Last Supper, Jesus reflected the vision of Jeremiah when he said: "This cup is God's New Covenant sealed with my blood" (Luke 22:20). For Christians, the solemn promise of Jeremiah had come to its fulfillment.

THE EXILIC PROPHETS

Ezekiel, Comforter of the Deported Judeans

When we enter the world of Ezekiel, we find ourselves in a strange and bizarre realm. The book seems excessively long with many repetitions. Some of Ezekiel's actions seem weird and childish; his symbolic and allegorical style is confusing, even frightening, to the reader. These various obstacles have made the Book of Ezekiel one of the most neglected parts of the Bible. But, to overlook Ezekiel would be tragic because this prophet provides several important insights into a renewal of Israel's religion.

In 598 B.C., the first group of Jerusalem's citizens were taken as captive exiles to Babylon. Most likely, Ezekiel was among the leaders of Judean society who suffered the humiliation of deportation to the land of their enemy. The son of a priest, he was probably trained for the priesthood at Jerusalem. His writings indicate an intense familarity with the Temple and its environs. But, when Ezekiel was forced to leave his home, his priestly career came to an end. We know nothing about his early years in captivity except that he was married and suffered the tragedy of his wife's death.

The Book is rather well organized. We can see the characteristic threefold pattern evident in other prophecies as well: (1) Ezekiel's call and his message of doom against Judah: chapters 1–24; (2) God's judgment on foreign nations: chapters 25–32 and (3) God's promises to his people for a hopeful future: chapters 33–48.

Ezekiel was a visionary with deep faith and a fertile imagination and some have questioned his mental stability. The distinguished philosopher and psychiatrist Karl Jaspers, for instance, believed that Ezekiel suffered from schizophrenia.

With Saul and several other Old Testament personalities, Ezekiel has undergone psychoanalysis "in absentia." In several psychology textbooks these figures are used as examples of persons whose effectiveness was diminished by personality disorders. It seems that it is impossible to analyze the mental state of Ezekiel, or any poet, using his writings alone. If we remember that symbols, visions and bizarre literary forms were used commonly in Ezekiel's day, it appears more likely that the Book of Ezekiel is the product of an unusually sensitive prophet, rather than the creation of a sick mind.

Ezekiel received his call to prophetism while in Babylon in 593 B.C. Chapters 1–3 indicate that it came in the midst of a thunderstorm in which he saw a chariot of God freely moving from place to place. This vision would be vitally important for Israel's faith in the future because it symbolized the insight that God was not subject to terrestrial boundaries.

Because Ezekiel and others proclaimed that God ruled every area of human life and that he was not limited to the Temple or the land of Judah, faith survived in the Exile. Jews could believe that their God was with them in Babylon or wherever they might live.

Like Jeremiah, Ezekiel ate the scroll containing the Word of God. This prophetic action symbolized that the Word permeated the prophet's life as he was appointed a watchman for the house of Israel and given responsibility for its spiritual survival.

Because his references to Jerusalem are so precise and detailed, some authors believed that Ezekiel may have returned to his native city and lived there during his days as a prophet. The weight of scholarly opinion, however, favors the view that he remained in Babylon during his entire ministry and lived at a place called Tel-Abib.

Until the fall of Jerusalem in 587 B.C., his ministry was directed to the city in the hope of waking its citizens to the seriousness of the times for the survival of faith. In the oracles directed against Jerusalem, Ezekiel portrays the history of Israel as one of continuous rebellion and sin against the Lord. Israel had customarily used the symbol of the vine to refer to the nobility of her election by God (Psalm 80). Ezekiel reversed the imagery and spoke of the vine as good only for firewood (Ezekiel 20:23–26).

When Jerusalem was destroyed, Ezekiel's oracles changed drastically. This offers an excellent witness to the transition from pre-exilic faith to post-exilic religion. The prophet dispelled the false notion that Israel's God was insular, focused on Israel alone, by showing that all history was under God's rule. In the midst of catastrophe, Ezekiel held out the hope that God had not abandoned his people. On the contrary, he saw the Exile as the occasion for the rejuvenation of a people now motivated by inner faith and no longer dependent upon the formal structures of a sacrificial cult.

Ezekiel frequently is called "the prophet of individualism." He did not advocate a rugged isolationism, but he stressed the responsibility of each person for his own salvation. With this insight, he helped his people put behind them the sins and infidelity of the past so that they could begin to build their future.

Perhaps Ezekiel learned a valuable lesson when Josiah's reform failed. He realized that reformation in faith is not imposed by law. True religion, for Ezekiel, was not a veneer, but an inner force rooted in steadfast loyalty to the Lord.

Israel needed not a superficial reform of cult but a radical reorientation of the ground of her being. Ezekiel saw the Exile as the gifted moment in which a renewed people could come to life. His celebrated vision of the Valley of Dry Bones (chapter 37) hopes for a new day for a renewed Israel.

Israel's shepherds, the kings and religious leaders, had failed. Now Ezekiel proclaimed that the Lord himself would shepherd his people (chapter 34). God alone was the author of Israel's salvation; he was the Good Shepherd. It was this image that the author of the Fourth Gospel employed when he spoke of Jesus as the Shepherd who gives his life for his flock (John 10).

Ezekiel, the semi-mystical dreamer, enabled the faith of Israel to move from a spirit of defeat to a hope for a resurrected people. He stands as one of the fathers of Judaism and a foundation for the Christian gospel. Both of these stress the importance of a religion "from the heart" and are optimistic about the future for a people who are not exempt from the trials of life but whose faith puts into perspective the whole human condition.

Second Isaiah (Isaiah 40–55)

For centuries it was thought that the oracles of Isaiah 40–55 were composed by Isaiah of Jerusalem. Although it was evident that these chapters reflected a time 150 years after Isaiah's death, Christians and Jews believed that the prophet was endowed with a special charism that enabled him to peer into the distant future. This was the opinion of the first Christians when they quoted these chapters in their New Testament.

Today, the common estimation of scholars is that these

chapters are not the work of the historical prophet Isaiah but, rather, reflect the message of a nameless sixth-century prophet who lived as an exile in Babylon. He spoke a message of hope to his people shortly after Babylon fell to Cyrus the Persian in 539 B.C. This prophet usually is designated as "Second Isaiah" or "Deutero-Isaiah" because his oracles were added to the scroll containing the prophecy of Isaiah of Jerusalem.

"Second Isaiah" tells us nothing about himself. Like his predecessor, Ezekiel, he shared the fate of the Exiles in Babylon. His oracles indicate that he knew the environment of Babylon from personal experience. A lyrical poet, Second Isaiah was the unchallenged spokesman for Israel's mission in the new era that dawned when Cyrus issued his edict allowing the captive Jews to return to Judah.

The language and style of his oracles breathe a spirit of optimism and vitality. As we reflect on his words, a broad horizon of new possibilities emerges for the People of God. Contemplating God's power in creation, the prophet praises the Father of Israel for his activity in salvation history.

It is likely that Second Isaiah was a successor of Isaiah's disciples. This school of prophecy kept the message of Isaiah alive and reinterpreted it in new situations. Certainly he exhibited the ability to use God's word creatively.

Second Isaiah's career spanned the years from the Fall of Jerusalem (587 B.C.) to those immediately before the Persian invasion of Babylon (539 B.C.). The Jewish exiles were living in a time of rapid political change. When Nebuchadnezzer died in 562 B.C., the Babylonian Empire began its steady decline, until Cyrus the Persian entered the city of Babylon in triumphant conquest.

Second Isaiah spoke on the eve of this decisive event. The prophet saw in the dramatic shift in history an evidence of God's sovereign control over human affairs. He viewed Cyrus as an instrument of the Lord's liberating power which would bring to an end the time of Exile. He went so far as to give Cyrus the title "Servant of the Lord." In this historical context, Second Isaiah reflected on the mission of Israel to the world.

Isaiah of Babylon announced an advent of God in human history. The Lord commanded the prophet to offer consolation to the exiles and to assure them that their days of bondage were over. The prophet imagined the return of his people to their homeland as a triumphant procession across the desert.

Jerusalem was styled as Judah's herald, proclaiming the coming of her God. Like Ezekiel's Vision of the Dry Bones, Second Isaiah's oracles look for a new creation of God's people, a time when God would be celebrated as the redeemer of Israel. Central to the prophet's faith in creation is a vibrant, hopeful vision for the days ahead.

Second Isaiah believed that Israel's liberation was imminent. In a glorious manifestation of his power, God would appear to his people to lead them home. Cyrus was the Lord's human agent who would break the yoke of Babylon and release the captives.

The gift of salvation is not for the Jews alone, however. It is meant to be shared by all peoples of the world. Deutero-Isaiah built on the theme of universalism in the prophet Amos. It was his hope that all people would derive life and freedom from the One God. The function of Israel in the world was to be a light to the nations so that salvation would reach to the end of the earth (Isaiah 49:6).

Second Isaiah's unique contribution to the Bible is found in his Servant Songs (42:1–4, 49:1–6, 50:4–9 and 52:13–53:12). They reflect the purpose and mission of the servant who suffers on behalf of his people, but who is finally exalted by his God. The identity of the servant is one of the most difficult questions in Old Testament exegesis. Sometimes he emerges as a single person, perhaps the prophet himself; at others it appears as if he represents the whole people of Israel.

Christians have used the servant imagery to portray the vicarious, redemptive sufferings of Jesus. It was largely this image that allowed the New Testament authors to come to terms with the apparent failure of Jesus' mission. The same figure helped the early Christians make sense of their own sufferings in the name of Jesus.

The Servant Songs highlight the mission of Israel to the people of the world. As servant, Israel is called to a responsibility for others. Hers is not a mission of self-serving privilege. Mark sums up the theme for the Christian Church when he records these words of Jesus: "For the Son of Man did not come to be served; he came to serve and to give his life to redeem many people" (Mark 10:45).

As an artist and prophet, Second Isaiah gave his people a vision of hope at a crucial juncture in their history. His words continue to offer us the consolation that God's creative power remains at work in our world. We are a new People of God, and yet our mission is the same as Israel's: to be a light to the nations.

POST-EXILIC PROPHETS

Cyrus's decree in 538 B.C. ended a generation of captivity and began a new chapter in the history of God's people. In the period immediately following it, several groups of Jews returned to Palestine to begin the arduous task of rebuilding their homeland.

The post-exilic community struggled against enormous odds. Economic problems, the failure of their crops and internal dissension about religious matters contributed to a spirit of depression. In addition, the exiles had to meet the hostility of the Samaritans who had remained in Palestine during the Exile. Many had intermarried with Assyrian and Babylonian colonists and were considered by the returning exiles to be religiously defiled.

When the Samaritans offered assistance in the rebuilding of the Jerusalem Temple, the offer was rebuffed. In their anger over this, the Samaritans began a campaign to sabotage the efforts of the Judeans to reconstruct their country. In the years that followed, relationships between Jews and Samaritans continued to deteriorate. With this background we can appreciate the radical nature of the parable in which Jesus made a good Samaritan a heroic model (Luke 10:29–37).

Prophecy continued among the Jewish people. Just as the Exilic prophets adapted their message in conditions in Babylon, the post-exilic prophets spoke God's word in a radically changed environment. Not only did they challenge Judah's citizens and encourage their efforts to rebuild the Temple, they also tried to give meaning to the internal convulsions that seemed ready to destroy the once powerful Persian empire.

Since the Persians seemed to have lost their grip on the empire, the post-exilic prophets hoped for a restoration of the Davidic dynasty in the person of Zerubbabel, the governor of Judah. We will consider the prophets Haggai, Zechariah and Malachi as examples of prophetism in the postexilic period.

Haggai

In 520 B.C. the exiles had been living in Jerusalem for some years, yet the Temple was still in ruins. The Book of Haggai represents the brief oracles of a man who encouraged leadership in the rebuilding effort. Delivered in 520 B.C., his words addressed Zerubbabel, the governor, and Joshua, the high priest, indicating that God was saying: "My people, why should you be living in well-built houses while my Temple lies in ruins?" (Haggai 1:4).

The prophet believed that the failure of the crops and the other problems the exiles were confronting were due to their neglecting to rebuild the Temple. In Deuteronomic style, Haggai was convinced that continued failure to heed the Lord's word would bring more poverty and starvation to Judah.

Soon after his oracles were delivered, the reconstruction effort began. Haggai bolstered the workers' confidence by assuring them of God's support. When, after a month's labor, enthusiasm began to wane, he promised a splendor for the new Temple that would surpass that of Solomon's edifice. He held out hope for a prosperity that would replace the prevalent poverty of the day.

In Haggai's oracles the reader encounters apocalyptic imagery for the first time in prophetism. Haggai speaks of the upheaval in the cosmic order and the overthrow of kingdoms which would result in Zerubbabel's being acknowledged as Messiah. It seems as if the spiritual and moral concerns of the previous prophets had given way to more pragmatic issues. Prophecy, in the traditional sense, was declining.

Zechariah

As a contemporary of Haggai, Zechariah shared the same concerns as his fellow prophet. Chapters 1–8 of his book reflect the oracles of the prophet delivered between 520 and 518 B.C. Chapters 9–14 are a collection of oracles from a later time. They are important for the development of messianic doctrine, styling the Messiah as a royal figure who is characterized by his humility.

Zechariah was greatly influenced by the prophet Ezekiel. Probably he was a priest and, like Haggai, he was preoccupied with the rebuilding of the Temple. He considered this the prelude to the Messianic Era. While he depicted Zerubbabel as a Davidic prince chosen by God to lead Judah to glory, it is clear in his oracles that God himself was the only source of Judah's hope. "You will succeed, not by military might or by your own strength, but by my spirit" (Zechariah 4:6).

The style of the book incorporates visions and highly symbolic language. The inroad of apocalyptic imagery is more evident than in Haggai.

Malachi

The pronouncements of Malachi reflect Jewish life in Palestine in about 450 B.C. The rebuilding of the Temple had been finished, yet the hope of the restored Jews was seriously threatened. The days of glory promised by Haggai and Zechariah had not materialized. Although the Temple was completed, economic hardship still plagued Judah. The messianic hope that had focused on Zerubbabel had been futile.

All events seemed to indicate that the Lord was not watching over the community in Judah. Priests' perfunctory duties were carried out in a spirit of boredom. Cheating and dishonesty characterized society. Mixed marriages and frequent divorce made the life style of the Jews fall short of the ideal of covenant faith.

In this environment the prophet Malachi spoke urging the people to renew their fidelity to the Lord. His messages were not delivered in oracular fashion. Rather, he used dialogue as his form of discourse, arguing his points in a logical sequence.

Malachi preached at a time when there was little respect

for the role of the prophet. He confronted his people whose lives had been marked by infidelity to the Covenant. His ministry paved the way for the later reforms initiated by Ezra and Nehemiah.

Third Isaiah

Most contemporary scholars hold that Isaiah 56–66 reflects the experiences of the post-exilic Judean community. Less hopeful than Second Isaiah, these chapters indicate that the conditions in which Judaism emerged were difficult for the People of God.

Compared with Isaiah 40–55, this section of the Isaian scroll, usually termed Third Isaiah or Trito-Isaiah, is less poetic. Its lack of unity indicates that it is the work of several individuals who were applying the message of Second Isaiah in new circumstances. Most likely, the prophecy is the product of the period following the ministries of Haggai and Zechariah.

The exiles who had returned from Babylon came to Judah with high hopes. The harsh realities of life quickly dashed their optimism. Third Isaiah's mission was to offer strength and vision to the post-exilic community and to proclaim the advent of a day of salvation for God's faithful ones. This same day would also spell condemnation for Judah's oppressors.

The prophet's image of God stresses his transcendence; yet, for Third Isaiah, God remains cognizant of the problems and desires of his people. A series of rhetorical questions in Isaiah 58:6–7 indicates that God is more concerned with authentic community life among the Jews than he is with precision in ritual or correct worship. His words serve to correct the overemphasis on the rubrics of the Temple and its cult made by his predecessors, Haggai and Zechariah.

The observance of fasts was criticized by Third Isaiah. The prophet indicated that God was oblivious to fasting because the people were indifferent to the needs of others. The fast desired by God would free the oppressed, care for the naked and hungry, be concerned for the poor and put aside contempt and slander. It would be characterized by a merciful attitude toward the needy (Isaiah 58:6–12).

Like Amos, Third Isaiah insisted that justice has priority over ritual observance. Prayer has its power in the context of charity. First place is given to a reverent attitude of humility before God which overflows in justice and love for persons.

In Isaiah 56–66 we see evidence of the emergence of apocalyptic literary style. This language drew a sharp distinction between the fates of the just and the unjust. Using symbolic and visionary language, it looked to the Lord to intervene on behalf of his people to establish a restored Jerusalem in which peace would reign.

Obadiah

Nothing is known about Obadiah, the author of the shortest book in the Old Testament. The book is unusual because of its vengeful polemic directed against the Edomites. The prophet looks forward to the Day of the Lord as a time of destruction for Edom.

Israel's hatred for Edom was firmly established. The rivalry between Jacob and Esau (Edom) is depicted in the pages of Genesis. When Jerusalem was attacked by Babylon in 597 B.C., Edom took the opportunity to exploit Judah in her time of peril. For her treachery, Obadiah welcomed a day of judgment for Edom.

The prophet describes the Day of the Lord as the time of God's wrath directed, not only against Edom, but on all pagan nations. Obadiah resembles other prophets in his mediating God's judgment on the nations; however, his vengeful nationalism is without equal in the Old Testament. He was motivated by an intense concern for the well-being of his people. His confidence was in God's sovereign power over all peoples. He may have been a man of violent temper; he was one of unwavering faith.

Joel

The Book of Joel represents the transition from prophetic to apocalyptic literature. Most authors believe it took form about 400 B.C. Unlike the Book of Daniel, which is not representative of prophetic literature and is categorized as apocalyptic, Joel stands among the prophets, yet his book contains the rudiments of the apocalyptic.

Joel's prophecy was occasioned by a locust plague that devastated the land of Judah. He viewed the calamity as a sign that the Day of the Lord was imminent and urged the people to proclaim a solemn fast as public penance for their sins.

Joel's words could be applicable to our Lenten observances. He asks that acts of repentance betoken a sincere return to the Lord: "Let your broken heart show your sorrow; tearing your clothes is not enough. Come back to the Lord your God. He is kind and full of mercy; he is patient and keeps his promise; he is always ready to forgive and not punish" (Joel 2:13).

Joel believed the Day of the Lord would bring a blessing and a time of plenty to a penitent people. To their pagan enemies, it would bring destruction for their past injuries to God's people.

The often quoted section referring to the pouring out of God's spirit (Joel 2:28) marks the beginning of the strongly apocalyptic section of the prophet's writings. In Joel 2:28–

3:21 he gives vivid details concerning the Day of the Lord: As a part of a cosmic upheaval, God's supremacy and Judah's prosperity will continue forever.

Typical of the post-exilic prophets, Joel is confident that God is the master of the universe. His sovereign rule will entail the ultimate prosperity of the now struggling remnant of Israel. It would have been natural for the prophets to have viewed their times with despair. To their credit, in the midst of adversity, they looked to the future with eyes focused on the promise of the Lord, confident that his people would not be abandoned.

The study of Israel's prophets must be more than an academic exercise or an excursion into history. Now, as in ancient days, the voice of prophetism should ring in the ears of every believer, calling him or her beyond the superficialities of religious affiliation to a faith that is the very fabric of life.

VI. The Writings

The Hebrew threefold division of Scripture employs its final category to group a miscellaneous collection of books that fail to find a place in the Torah or in the Prophets. Because of its diverse character, it is almost impossible to make any general comments about this classification that would be applicable to all of the books found in the Writings. The spectrum ranges from the hymns of the Psalms to the visions of Daniel, from the skepticism of Ecclesiastes to the celebration of human love in the Song of Songs.

For the sake of order we will begin with a consideration of the Wisdom Tradition in Israel. Next, we will view the Psalms as Israel's expressions of worship. The books of Esther, Ruth and Jonah are presented as correctives to an insular and excessively elitest mentality which developed in post-exilic Judaism. Finally, our attention will turn to the closing years of the Old Testament era as we consider the period of Greek persecution which spawned the Maccabean revolt and the Book of Daniel.

THE WISDOM OF THE SAGES

The prophet Jeremiah records the words of his opponents: "Let's do something about Jeremiah! There will always be priests to instruct us, wise men to give us counsel, and prophets to proclaim God's message" (Jeremiah 18:18). This verse mentions three groups that influenced the lives of the Israelites. Israel's priests were the interpreters of the Law. Its prophets were spokesmen for the Lord, calling the people back to the purity of Mosaic faith. Finally, it was the function of the Wiseman, or Sage, to offer practical advice on the issues and problems of the day.

From these ancient sages emerged a major body of Old Testament literature, the Wisdom Writings. Known for their talent in understanding human problems, the men of wisdom, together with the priests and prophets, were the shapers of Israelite thought.

Even before the birth of Greek philosophy, the Hebrew sages reflected on the profound mysteries of life. The Wisdom Movement had a timeless quality. Although some of the ancient wisdom literature dates back to the Age of the Pyramids (2600–2200 B.C.), most of Israel's wisdom tradition is the product of the five centuries before the Christian era.

The Roman Catholic Canon of Scripture lists six books in the Wisdom category: Proverbs, Job, Ecclesiastes or Qoheleth, Song of Songs, Book of Wisdom and Ecclesiasticus or Sirach. Sometimes one finds the Psalms listed as Wisdom Literature; however, most authors treat them in a class by themselves.

Even a superficial reading of one of these books leaves the impression that the Wisdom tradition differs greatly from the Old Testament Law and Prophets. With the exception of a section of Ecclesiasticus, the idea of Salvation History is absent. The great events and heroes that constitute the story of Israel are not mentioned. In other sections of the Old Testament the Exodus looms clear in almost every book. In the Wisdom Literature, reference to the great event that formed the Israelites is hardly evident.

Unlike the writings of the prophets, this literature did not address institutional religion. Nor did it speak to Israel as a community of faith. Rather, the concern of the sages was the individual person. Authors in other areas of Hebrew Scripture traced the history of God's salvational activity in Israel's past. The Wisdom writers sought to analyze the question of human existence on its deepest level. In this sense, it is more philosophical than theological.

Israel's sages did not begin with Revelation to explain the meaning of life. Instead, the discipline, intelligence and moral behavior of man was their springboard for discussion. Equipped with keen powers of observation, the wisemen were to instruct the youth on the key to a successful and happy life. Their method was empirical and existential. The scope of their concern was not limited by the boundaries or religion of Israel. Writing with an international flavor, Israel's sages tackled the problems every person faces: suffering, injustice, reward and retribution, to name but a few.

Wisdom, in the Hebrew tradition, was regarded as a gift from God. Even though scholars cannot pinpoint the origins of the Wisdom movement in Israel, it is clear that the people believed a special charism from the Lord was with the sage as he delivered his message at the city gate.

Because of his patronage of arts and literature, King Solomon became a symbol of Wisdom. In fact, several sections of the Wisdom Literature are attributed to him. The popular story about Solomon's decision in the case of the two women who claimed the same child (First Kings 3:16–28) has been used as evidence that God had given Solomon the gift of wisdom in response to the King's prayer for an "understanding heart" (First Kings 3:3–14).

For the sake of study, the Wisdom Literature can be divided into two general types. Prudential Wisdom was influenced by Egyptian philosophy. Its chief concern was to teach the young how to live the good life. By nature it was conservative and practical. Its outlook was optimistic and frequently its doctrine was encapsulated in short, witty statements. The Book of Proverbs best represents this type of Wisdom.

The second group might be termed "reflective." It was influenced by Mesopotamian literature and was more critical in thrust. Typified by the Book of Job and Ecclesiastes, these works asked serious questions about the meaning and purpose of life. The authors often assumed the posture of radical skepticism in order to make the reader think deeply about the basic issues of human existence. This literature was more pessimistic and frequently employed the form of dialogue, as in Job. In an indirect way, the Biblical books in this category are asking radical questions about the meaning of true religion. The very foundations of human knowledge are explored with a critical eye.

Face to face with life's mysteries, the sages expressed their humility. Although they explored the meaning of human existence, they in the end admitted that it was God's universe and that he was in control of our destiny. The wiseman spoke of the Fear of the Lord as the beginning of wisdom. By this he meant that human speculation begins and ends by acknowledging God's place in the human scene.

Because of their great compassion and understanding of people, the sages attracted a following in Israel. In a real sense, they mediated the Law and the Prophets to the common folk. Their broad universalism and liberality of thought were preparation for the gospel of Jesus. We will now turn our attention to four representative books in the Wisdom tradition that show this.

The Book of Proverbs

The Book of Proverbs is the oldest written representative of the Wisdom Movement in Israel. Its rich variety demonstrates the broad spectrum of the sages' concerns and interests. The book might be classified as an anthology that depicts the rich diversity of the Wisdom Literature. Proverbs closely resembles collections of Egyptian wisdom writings and, like its counterparts, it both served an educational purpose and challenged its readers to explore the issues of life in a profound way.

Proverbs assumes that human beings have the native ability to make their lives successful and happy. Essentially optimistic in tone, it indicates that the person who heeds the instruction of the sages will have security in life.

The basic literary unit of the book, the *mashal*, or parable, was written for young men to assist their growth in a personal moral sense and in practical wisdom. Its opening verses state this purpose well: "Here are proverbs that will help you recognize wisdom and good advice, and understand sayings with deep meaning. They can teach you how to live intelligently and how to be honest, just and fair. They can make an inexperienced person clever and teach young men how to be resourceful" (Proverbs 1:2–4).

Like the rest of the Wisdom Literature, Proverbs makes no mention of Israel's past. The great themes of Salvation History are absent. Proverbs' pointed verses indicate what course of action will be followed by the wise man in such diverse areas of life as family relationships, business dealings and social etiquette.

For its author, virtue is the key to a successful human life. Emphasis is placed on man's responsibility for his fate rather than on God's salvational acts in human history. Yet, the basis of Israel's wisdom is stated in Proverbs 9:10: "To be wise you must first have reverence for the Lord. If you know the Holy One, you will have understanding."

In two sections of the Book of Proverbs, Proverbs 1:20–33 and 8:1–9:6, wisdom is pictured with human attributes. Personified wisdom introduced a new theological perspective in the Old Testament. Wisdom was represented as having an eternal existence. She was active in creation and had the prerogative of sustaining all that the Lord has made. In time, Lady Wisdom came to be associated with a divine message or even identified with God himself.

The author of the fourth Gospel built on this theme when he spoke of God's Word as a person. He says of Jesus: "The Word was the source of life, and this life brought light to mankind" (John 1:4).

Although much of Proverbs reflects pedestrian concerns, its contents yield a rich treasure that paved the way for the statement that reflects the mystery and miracle of Christian faith: "The Word became a human being and, full of grace and truth, lived among us" (John 1:14).

The Song of Songs

The person with a puritanical mind will have difficulty accepting the Song of Songs as part of the Bible. Named in a Hebrew form that expresses a superlative, it represents a collection of lyrics, often quite explicitly erotic, celebrating the delights of the love of a man and a woman.

This folk literature views human sexuality as a part of the divine plan for the fully integrated person. The Song extols the beauty of nature and the bounties of God's creation. Although the book has no explicitly religious content, its theological meaning is evident if we grant the premise that human love is a reflection of God's love for his people.

Because the Song of Songs had difficulty being officially recognized as part of the Hebrew Bible, it has been attributed to King Solomon, the patron of Israel's Wisdom Movement. Pious sensitivities no doubt were offended by the lyrics' sensual imagery. The Rabbi Akiba, at the Jewish Council of Jamnia (circa: A.D. 90), insisted that the Song of Solomon offered insights into the relationship of God and his people. Centuries earlier, the prophet Hosea had spoken of God's covenant with mankind in terms of a marriage, with Israel as the Lord's bride.

There is no Old Testament basis for Hellenistic dualism separating persons into body and soul components. The Song of Songs is no exception to the rule. It depicts man as a body-person in the totality of his humanity. Men and women are fulfilled in their union and married love is a reflection of the goodness of God's love. For this reason, the verses of the Song were frequently used at wedding celebrations.

Discovering the Song of Songs in our bibles is a strong reminder that, for a people who believe that God is the Creator of all things, nothing is "common" or "ordinary." It is not we who make all things sacred; rather, all things were created holy by their Creator.

Job

For the person who feels that certitude is the bedrock of faith, the Book of Job will be an embarrassment. In an effort to think deeply on the dilemmas of faith, its author has called into question certain pious assumptions held by the believers of his day. The result is a book that has a timeless relevance to anyone who realizes the difficulties of belief. Since faith often produces more questions than answers, the Book of Job attempts to explore faith from the realistic point of view that belief is a relationship between persons, a relationship that is marked with a high degree of probability and ambiguity on the part of the believer.

Many commentators feel that Job is the outstanding example of the Wisdom Literature in Israel. Its author must have had a deeply religious relationship with God. He was sensitive to the plight of human suffering and tragedy. Although his identity is lost in history, he was a genius as a theologian and poet. The word "author" may be misleading. Interpreters agree that the Book of Job is the product of several persons and editing processes.

The Book of Job probably employed an ancient story as a framework to offer a serious challenge to the conventional piety of the day. It is a tale of a just man, noted for his goodness, who suffers one tragedy after another until his life is in complete ruin.

Job's friends enter the story to explain his sufferings in terms of the traditional religious values. They assume that God rewards the good deeds of people and that the world is the forum where wickedness is punished. Their assumption reflects the attitudes of an Israel who had yet to believe in life after death as survival of the person.

His friends urge Job to acknowledge his sin; yet Job, realizing his innocence, could not understand how God could visit tragedy upon him. When he became aware that the ways of God do not correspond to human patterns he repented and acknowledged God's power with humility. In the end, he was restored to even greater fortune and wealth, while God reprimanded his friends for their superficial explanations of Job's suffering.

The Book of Job represents a revolt against the religious principles that would try to answer the problem of suffering by reason alone. Saint Paul built on the insight of Job when he wrote, "We know that in all things God works for good with those who love him, those he has called according to his purpose" (Romans 8:28).

We encounter in Job the rejection of absolute applications of the principle of reward and punishment. The author does not set aside moral principles, but he does shun the tendency to categorize all human experience. Jesus seems to have shared these same perspectives (Luke 13:1–3 and John 9:1–3).

The drama of Job confronts the reader with the fact that

faith is often a journey in the darkness of uncertainty and doubt. The problem of suffering is never dismissed or explained away. Job indicates that it is possible for a person to confess faith in a wise and loving God in spite of the tragedy and unequality of human existence.

For the Christian, the Cross and Resurrection of Jesus take us beyond the Book of Job. Through the eyes of Resurrection, faith, suffering and tragedy are not welcomed, but they are given meaning. The thrust of Christian belief tells us that if we share in Jesus' death we will partake in his victory.

Ecclesiastes

The optimism of the Wisdom Movement stands in stark contrast with the pessimistic view of life presented by the philosopher-author of Ecclesiastes. Sometimes called Qoheleth, "the teacher," the author assumes the posture of a critic and probes the established view of life to expose its weakness and superficial stance. Using the method of the Wisdom Movement, Qoheleth differs from the popular sages and offers a series of challenges to Hebrew religion.

Written in the third or fourth century B.C., Ecclesiastes recognizes that one of the fruits of wisdom is to recognize the limitations of human knowledge. In his honest view of life, he saw the folly of man's finite intellect trying to discover the infinite wisdom of God.

Using the form of personal musings, the book begins and ends on a skeptical note. "It is useless, useless, said the Philosopher. Life is useless, all useless. You spend your life working, laboring, and what do you have to show for it?" (Ecclesiastes 1:2).

Like the author of Job, Qoheleth realized the futility of attempting to discern the plan of God. He preached resignation to the harsh and sometimes cruel facts of life. He preferred this approach to the vapid, complacent and hollow piety he witnessed in religious thinkers.

Qoheleth's real contribution to religious faith is his radical questioning. His constant probing reminds us that the quest for wisdom is never-ending. Perhaps the key to a solid faith is not to think one has all the answers, but to realize that there are genuine questions to be raised. Frequently, "religious people" ignore the contradictions between their belief and the facts of life. This Book indicates that a faith that cannot be intelligently examined will not stand the test of life's dilemmas.

Today, Ecclesiastes challenges superficial piety. It presents the believer with an opportunity to redefine and rethink his or her faith commitment to the Lord.

THE PSALMS, THE PRAISES OF ISRAEL

Experts in the field of comparative religion tell us that a reliable index of a people's religious belief is found in the prayers they have composed. For the ancient Israelite, the Psalm was a favorite type of prayer.

A biblical collection of 150 of these prayers survives in the Book of Psalms. For centuries, this Prayer Book of Israel has been a vehicle for people to address God. While praying the Psalms, millions have meditated on God's loving fidelity to his people. In the Psalms we encounter the broad spectrum of a covenant-relationship between God and Israel. As the Israelite prayed, he or she gave voice to Hebrew faith in a saving God. At prayer, the People of God related all aspects of life, its pleasure and pain, joy and sorrow, to the Creator and Sustainer of life.

Martin Luther, referring to the Psalter as the Bible in miniature, wrote that all areas of Hebrew life and faith were reflected in the Psalms. Today, when we pray the Psalms, we are inserted into the drama of Israel's Salvation History.

It is impossible to pinpoint the exact origin of the Psalms. They reflect the Old Testament period from the time of David (1000 B.C.) to the days just before the dawn of the Christian era. Most likely, the 150 Psalms in our Bible represent a selection from many more Psalms that were composed during this period.

It is probable that the Psalter was the hymnbook used in the Second Jerusalem Temple, which was built in the sixth century B.C. Like modern hymnals, it contains religious songs for diverse occasions and festivals, taken from several periods of the people's history. The fact that most of the Psalms were composed for a cultic purpose has given us great insight into Israel's prayer and worship.

For centuries it was believed that King David was the author of the Psalms. Today, we realize that, although the Psalter may be dedicated to the great King of Israel, he is not their author. The Psalms came into existence over a period of several centuries.

In Hebrew, the Psalms are called "Tehillim," a word that means "praises." Whether they were occasioned by joy or misfortune, each hymn was viewed as a song celebrating the glory of God. The faith of the psalmist colored his total view of life. Helmer Ringgren, a noted authority on the subject, labels this faith "theocentric piety."

An additional characteristic of the psalmist's faith was its communitarian dimension. For the Hebrew, prayer was the loving response of an entire people to their God. What may have been the plaintive song of an individual's suffering (e.g., Psalm 38) became a psalm of the whole community in praise of the Savior God. A contemporary Christian whose main conception of prayer is an individual's communication with God will never be able to pray the Psalms with real meaning or feeling.

The poetic quality of song leads us to expect the language of poetry in the Psalms. They must be encountered on their own terms, with all the figures of speech one normally would expect in hymns or religious songs.

In the early decades of the century, giant strides were made in the field of psalm research. H. Gunkel, in his investigations, divided the Psalter according to several types of psalms he found there. He and other scholars stressed the connection of the Psalms with the worship of Israel. Their categories have been refined over the years; yet, it is still helpful to study a psalm with reference to its group or class. The main categories are laments, hymns, liturgical psalms, royal psalms and wisdom psalms.

The laments reflect a worshipping people in the midst of some misfortune. They may be voiced by an individual or by the entire community of Israel. Psalm 79 is a lament over the fall of Jerusalem sung by all the people. In Psalm 6 an individual reflects on his personal suffering and asks God to rescue him from affliction. Each lament contains a section which is termed "certainty of a hearing." Here the author expresses faith that God has heard his prayer and will eventually rescue him from the danger that threatens.

Psalm 113 represents a Hymn of Praise. These hymns extol the Lord for his majestic benevolence to his creatures. This type of psalm usually begins and ends with an invitation to praise the Lord. It is characterized by a narration of God's saving acts for his people.

Liturgical psalms are those whose content clearly indicates that they were employed in the public worship of Israel. They frequently speak of festivals and pilgrimages connected with the Temple. Zion, or Jersualem, is featured as God's Holy Mountain and journey to the City is described. Psalms 76 and 122 are examples of liturgical psalms.

Royal psalms are generous in their praise of the king. They affirm his close relationship with God, and most reflect hope for Israel's future. Because of their frequent mention of the king as "God's anointed one," they are sometimes called "messianic psalms."

Psalm 89 is based on the prophet Nathan's confrontation of King David with his sin. Closely related to this group are Psalms 47, 93 and 95–99, which celebrate the Kingship of God. They focus on hope for the future rule of God over the entire world. These psalms are important background for the New Testament concept of the Kingdom of God.

Finally, the Wisdom Psalms reflect a more philosophical attitude toward life. They contrast the fate of the righteous with that of the ungodly. Psalm 37 and Psalm 1, the prologue to the Psalter, are both wisdom psalms and are closely related to the Wisdom Literature of the Old Testament.

The Book of Psalms provides a unique insight into the relationship of Israel to the Lord. Reflecting diverse aspects of life, these songs witness to the faith response of a people who realized the centrality of God in their community.

When we pray the Psalms today, we realize that we stand in continuity with the people of faith. We worship the same God, whose wondrous deeds were praised in their religious songs.

VII. Bridging the Testaments

The last centuries of the Old Testament era brought turmoil and a period of persecution to the people of Israel. At first, Judeans who resettled the area around Jerusalem prospered under the benevolent administration of their Persian overlords. From 539 to 332 B.C. Israel enjoyed a measure of freedom as the city of Jerusalem was rebuilt to become once again the center of the nation's government and religious devotion. In 332 B.C. the Persian dominions came under the control of the Greeks with the mighty world conquest of Alexander from Macedon. The period of Greek control, which lasted until 63 B.C., saw the faith of Israel severely tested. The last books of the Old Testament came to birth during this time of persecution.

Biblical history for most of these centuries cannot be reconstructed with precision. Ezra's reform in the fourth century B.C. is the last event recorded in the Books of Ezra and Nehemiah. Almost two hundred years follow before the Scriptures resume the story of Israel in I and II Maccabees. The Maccabean literature has its setting in the second century B.C.

In the books of Esther, Ruth and Jonah we read three short stories that provide insight into the struggle of God's people to come to grips with their Gentile domination. A crucial issue for them was how they could maintain their identity, which was threatened in a pagan world, and still be conscious of their God-given vocation of being a light to the Gentiles. The complexity of the times is evident in the pages of these books. Each indicates that the era of domination was the crucible in which a new understanding of God's call to Israel took form.

ESTHER AND RUTH

As an historical novel set in the Persian era, the Book of Esther stressed that the Jews must separate from the world of the Gentiles to insure their religious identity. Often insular and vindictive in tone, the story of Esther resembles the nationalism of the prophet Nahum. The book was intended to encourage believers as they faced overwhelming oppression from hostile intruders. A secondary motive for the author's work was to account for the popular Jewish festival of Purim.

Esther, whose Hebrew name was Hadassah, was a beautiful Jewish woman who became the wife of Ahasuerus, or Xerxes, the king of Persia from 486 to 465 B.C. As Queen of Persia, Esther courageously risked her life to prevent a pogrom initiated to destroy her people.

The Book of Esther is unique in that God is not mentioned in its pages and religious matters are nowhere in evidence. In the Septuagint version there is expressed the belief that God has called Israel to be a people separate from the rest of the world. For the Jewish people Esther remains a heroine of faith. She was the valiant woman who placed the good of her people above her concern for her own life.

To protect its life from contamination from pagan cults

and values, Israel was forced to isolate itself from the Gentile world. In this atmosphere Jewish attitudes became exclusive and somewhat vindictive toward pagans. To correct the imbalance, the Book of Ruth offered for Israel's consideration a pagan woman whose faith prompted her to join herself to Israel.

The Book of Ruth recalls the story of a Moabite woman from the era of the Judges who became a member of the family of Israel and, ultimately, the great-grandmother of King David.

Part of Ezra's attempt to preserve the purity of Jewish faith was to forbid marriages between Jews and Gentiles. His decrees went as far as to dissolve such marriages that already existed. Perhaps the Book of Ruth was written to protest his policy. In idyllic form it is the fictional account of Ruth's marriage to a Hebrew who dies leaving her without children. Upon his death, Ruth chose to go to Judah with her Hebrew mother-in-law, Naomi. Another Hebrew, Boaz, became enchanted with her kindness and fidelity. He married her and became the father of her children.

In a day of exclusiveness, the story of Ruth served to remind the people of God that Israel had no monopoly on God's love and concern. The Book of Jonah takes up this same theme by satirizing the attitudes of the Jewish leaders who were advocates of isolationism.

JONAH, THE RELUCTANT PROPHET

Unlike other biblical prophecies, the Book of Jonah is not a collection of oracles. It is a story about a prophet who is reluctant to carry out his mission. Popular interpretation often mentions "Jonah and the whale"; yet, a whale is not part of the story.

The author intended to point out the foolishness of

Jonah's attitude, an attitude shared by many in the post-exilic community. The satirical nature of the book and its humorous episodes do not detract from its deep theological insights on the universal character of God's mercy.

Post-exilic exclusiveness tended to underscore Israel's election as God's privileged people. Hostility toward the Samaritans was fostered. Narrow nationalism and religious bigotry became typical attitudes in Judah.

It seems that the Book of Jonah was written as a protest against these developments, which the author believed to be contrary to Mosaic faith. Sometime between 400 and 200 B.C., the author told his parable to remind Israel of her responsibilities to nations that did not share her faith. The Book of Jonah underscores the Lord's concern and mercy as having a universal dimension.

As the Book of Jonah begins, the prophet is called by God to preach in the Assyrian capital of Nineveh. His task is to announce the fall of the corrupt city. Unwilling to accept his mission, Jonah boarded a ship going in the opposite direction. A violent storm threatened the safety of the boat and its passengers. Jonah realized that the storm was the result of his disobedience, so he suggested that the sailors toss him into the sea. When they did, the sea became calm. The reluctant prophet was promptly swallowed by a huge fish which ferried him to the shore and vomited him onto the beach.

By this time Jonah realized that God was serious. When the Lord called him a second time to go to Nineveh, he promptly obeyed the summons. As he entered the great city, he called its citizens to repent and turn to the Lord. Imagine his shock when all the inhabitants, from the king to the lowest servant, did penance for their sins. God heard their prayers and revoked his sentence of doom.

Jonah was angered at the Ninevites' response to his preaching. He begrudged God's willing pardon of these

Gentile sinners. Preferring death rather than witnessing God's favor extended to these pagans, the petulant prophet withdrew from the city, constructed a shelter and waited to see what would happen next.

God gave Jonah a large plant to protect him from the desert sun; but soon he sent a worm to devour it. Now Jonah lamented the death of his protective plant and said he would be better off dead. God addressed an angry prophet: "The plant grew up in one night and disappeared the next; you didn't do anything for it and you didn't make it grow—yet, you feel sorry for it! How much more, then, should I have pity on Nineveh, that great city. After all, it has more than 120,000 innocent children in it, as well as many animals!" (Jonah 4:10–11).

The central message of this short story is close to the Gospel proclaimed by Jesus. Both give emphasis to the universal nature of God's love. As in the parable of the Prodigal Son, the God of Jonah is generous in his pardon and forgiveness. Like the parable of the Good Samaritan, the Book of Jonah exemplifies the willingness of foreigners to respond to the God of Israel.

Throughout Salvation History, the People of God seemed obstinate in their failure to appreciate the Lord's covenant promises; yet, the Ninevites responded to God's offer of forgiveness with spontaneous enthusiasm.

Second Isaiah had spoken of Israel's responsibility in terms of "a light for the Nations." The author of Jonah reinforces this theme when he indicates that Jonah has the obligation of telling foreigners that God loves them and is concerned for them. The reality of Nineveh's sins is obvious; yet, admirable qualities are also evident among these pagans. Like the Book of Ruth, Jonah stands in contrast to a narrow mentality that would set boundaries to the Lord's love and pardon.

Jonah's attitudes are sometimes reflected in contemporary Christians. While we laugh at Jonah's narrow-mindedness, we might do well to examine our own feelings. Because God's loving care extended to all his creatures, we cannot set limits on his generous forgiveness. The Book of Jonah would remind us that Christians have no monopoly on goodness and that there is no person so bad that we can dismiss him or her.

Each person, like Jonah, has a Nineveh—that impossible situation that seems beyond our abilities or concern. We, like the Reluctant Prophet, are frequently the Lord's voice, calling his people to himself. The Book of Jonah draws our attention to Jesus' wish that his church be his witness to all people, even to the ends of the earth.

JEWISH RESISTANCE TO HELLENISM; THE MACCABEAN REVOLT

When Alexander the Great died in 323 B.C., he left no male heir; thus, his vast empire was divided among his four generals. Two strong dynasties emerged from the partition and affected the course of Jewish history. The Ptolemies controlled the area of Egypt. Their holdings initially included the land of the Jews. Syria and its environs fell to the domination of the Seleucids. In 198 B.C., the Seleucid king, Antiochus III, wrested control of Israel from the Ptolemies. From that date to the beginnings of Roman rule the Jews were stringently ruled by the Syrian Hellenists.

Antiochus IV, Epiphanes (175–163 B.C.) came to the throne when his brother was assassinated. One of his goals was to find new sources of revenue so that Rome could be appeased and the Syrian territory kept free from the advance of Roman armies. In addition, Antiochus IV wanted to unify the diverse people he governed. He sought to do so by forcing his subjects to adopt the same culture. Be-

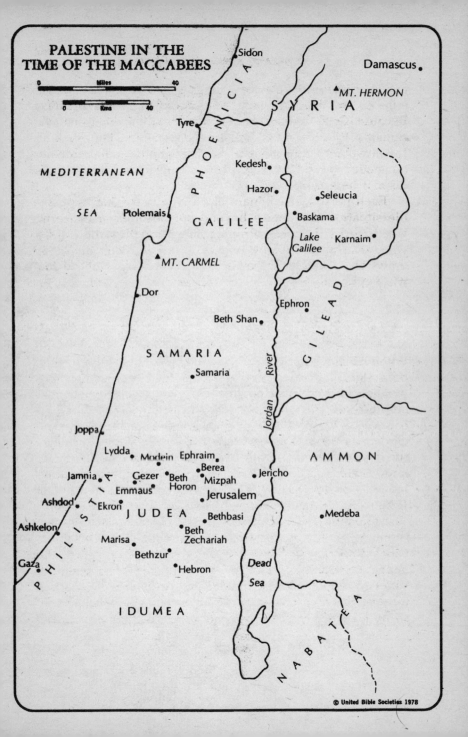

cause he plundered the Jerusalem Temple treasury and sought to make worship of Greek gods mandatory in Judea, zealous Jews viewed Antiochus IV as an enemy of their faith.

Not all Jews were opposed to his policies. Many appropriated the Hellenistic ways and went so far as to worship the Greek gods. When Antiochus built a gymnasium in Jerusalem, it attracted Jewish men even though the cult of Greek deities was intimately associated with the sports program. Hellenizers were especially prevalent in the upper classes of Judean society.

In the midst of this new threat to Judaism, a revival movement was born. It rekindled the Mosaic faith in the hope of establishing a new kingdom of Israel. Called the Hasidim, or "pious ones," these Jews came from the more rural areas where they had remained relatively free from the infection of Hellenism. They urged their fellow Jews to shun the Hellenistic influences. Most scholars view them as predecessors of the Pharisees whom Jesus encountered in his ministry.

Claiming to be the incarnation of the Greek god Zeus, Antiochus IV conspired to control the office of Jewish High Priest. He made the observance of Jewish law and ritual a crime. Circumcision was forbidden and those caught observing Jewish festivals and sabbaths were liable for death. In 168 B.C. the Greek army marched into Jerusalem and desecrated the Temple by erecting an altar to Zeus in its sacred precinct and offering pigs, animals unclean according to Jewish law, as sacrifices before the altar. This horrible crime earned the Jewish appellation "Abomination of Desolation." Jewish society was ripe for rebellion.

In Modein, a town to the northwest of Jerusalem, the citizens were being forced to offer sacrifice to the pagan deities. Mattathias, a priest in that village, refused to take part in the rituals. In a moment of anger he killed a Jew who came forward to sacrifice and a Syrian officer who was charged with enforcing Antiochus's order. Mattathias and his five sons fled to the Judean hill country where a band of the Hasidim joined them. As Mattathias was dying, he entrusted the cause of rebellion to his son, Judas. To acknowledge his zeal, Judas was given the name Maccabeus. The word is usually taken to mean "hammerer." The Maccabean revolt raged against tremendous odds. Judas and his companions defeated the Syrian armies and took control of Jerusalem. In 165 B.C. he recaptured the Temple area, destroyed the pagan shrine and reconsecrated the Temple in a joyous festival in which the building was illumined by oil lamps. The Jewish celebration of Hanukkah, or Rededication, observed in the month of December, commemorates this triumph of the Maccabees.

The Maccabean revolt won autonomy for the Jews. A measure of freedom was restored until the Roman army conquered Judea in 63 B.C. In the light of the revolt, it is understandable that the Romans were concerned when Jesus was proclaimed "King of the Jews." The failure of the Syrio-Greek forces during the days of the Maccabees led Roman authorities to be suspicious of any popular leader among the Jews who might be the catalyst for a revolt against Roman rule.

DANIEL,
THE EMERGENCE OF APOCALYPTIC STYLE

A profound challenge to the faith of Israel came to a head in the Maccabean era. Hellenism threatened to wipe out the distinctive faith and culture of the Jewish people. To reinforce Mosaic faith, the Hasidic movement stressed the necessity of unwavering loyalty to Israel's God, even in the midst of tyrannical persecution. It is the Book of Daniel that gave flesh to the theology of the Maccabean era. Several experts have called it the "Manifesto of the Hasidim." The author of Daniel cleverly used incidents from Israel's past to typify the faith and loyalty God required during the painful Hellenistic period.

Although the book was written in the last years of the Old Testament times, its setting is in the Babylonian Exile of the sixth century B.C. Some people who supposed the book was written during the Exile have misunderstood its nature, viewing it as a forecast of future events. This mistake led compilers of English bibles to place Daniel among the prophetic books. The Hebrew listing correctly includes Daniel in the category of the Writings.

Countless people, sometimes of fanatical bent, have used the Book of Daniel as a source for every manner of prediction concerning the future. Indeed, some have attempted to discern the whole course of future religious history in its pages. As in the case of the New Testament Book of Revelation, the misunderstanding of Daniel has led many commentators to distort its meaning severely.

The author of Daniel intended to speak to the Jews of his own era, offering a measure of support and encouragement in their time of trial by recalling a similar period in Israel's past in which God's guiding hand did not fail his people. He wrote under the guise of speaking from the past to the future rather than from the present into the past. Daniel's usage of persons and events from the past, who were practically unknown to the Greeks, did not incur their displeasure. If the book had spoken directly against the tyranny of the Seleucids it would have been suppressed immediately. In the second century B.C., when the days of the prophets were thought to be over, it was a common practice for authors to write under the name of some figure from Israel's ancient tradition—in this case, Daniel.

To grasp the message of Daniel it is important to understand the literary form in which the book is cast. Daniel belongs to a type of Biblical literature called apocalyptic. As the era of prophecy was drawing to a close, apocalyptic writing emerged as a new style. The word apocalyptic means "uncovering." Its central theme is the coming of God's kingdom as a time of fulfillment of God's promises to his people. Characteristic of apocalyptic style are bizarre visions, the extensive usage of symbols and an emphasis on the world of the supernatural. Its language is a type of code that makes its meaning accessible only to the faithful. For others, an apocalyptic book was not understood.

Apocalyptic literature flourished in times of persecution. As Daniel arose during the Hellenistic persecution of the Jews, its New Testament counterpart, the Book of Revelation, was written as the Christian community faced opposition from the Jews and the Roman government.

Paradoxical themes of hope and despair are prominent in Daniel. While the author sees the course of human history as leading to ruin, he expresses a fervent hope that God's power continues to act in the world he fashioned. The Book of Daniel envisions a divine plan whereby the terrors of history would climax with a divine intervention to transform the earth into a perfect world where God's faithful ones would be rewarded for their loyalty and his enemies would perish. Frequently, the reader of apocalyptic literature encounters a vindictive prayer for the damnation of the enemies who oppress the faithful.

The Book of Daniel can be divided into two main sections. The first, chapters 1–6, contains stories about Daniel, who represents God's judgment on the events of the world. When threatened with death, he and his friends display extraordinary courage and their fidelity to God evokes the admiration of both believers and pagans. The story of the youths in the fiery furnace and Daniel in the lions' den typify this section. Section 2, chapters 7–12, is composed of four visions of Daniel. Chapter 7 confesses that God will triumph over the wickedness of this world and give his kingdom to a figure standing between heaven and earth called the Son of Man. A forecast of the future of the biblical lands for the time after the Exile is found in chapter 8. Chapter 9 contains Daniel's powerful prayer in which he places trust in the Lord in spite of adversity. It is followed by a divine promise that the faithful will be victorious. Finally, chapters 10–12 contain a visionary account of a great struggle of the pious ones with an evil king. The conflict will result in the end of the present age.

To enter the world of Daniel is to confront the bewildering concepts of apocalyptic literature. Our temptation might be to dismiss the book as irrelevant for our time. Yet, the cruelty of our age and our confrontation with massive forces of evil beyond our abilities to identify clearly, lead the person of faith to renew his or her belief that God has not deserted his people and that his plan for the world will not fail. For the Christian, Daniel, written less than two centuries before the dawn of the Christian era, provides an insight into an important avenue of Jewish thinking which had a serious impact on the New Testament. Also, for us Jesus is the answer to Daniel's visions and prayers. In Christ, God's plan continues and we become part of Salvation History.

Conclusion

In these pages we have traced the course of Salvation History through the Old Testament. Beginning with Genesis, we met a God who created out of generosity. He is a God totally in love with his people and yet those people often matched his fidelity by their sin and betrayal. God did not give up on them, nor did he abandon them to their sins. He intervened, often dramatically, as in the Exodus, to assure the salvation of his beloved. He raised up great leaders, like the Judges and the Kings. As a father who must correct erring children, he sent his prophets in the hope of evoking steadfast love from his people. When their kingdoms were in ruins and they were living in exile, God journeyed with them to remind them again of his devotion and love. Through the sages and psalmists he offered his people a vision of steadfast love that could overcome their hatred, greed and selfishness. Finally, in an era of great suffering, when it seemed as if the People of God faced extinction, God spoke again through people like the Maccabees and Daniel to bolster the faith and trust of Israel.

As we read the Old Testament we are not impartial observers or uninvolved spectators. We see ourselves reflected in its words. The God that Jesus revealed to us is the God of the Patriarchs, Moses, the prophets, the psalmists, Daniel and, most importantly, the God of all those nameless people of faith who responded to his love. We can become more aware of the Lord's working in our own salvation histories as we see him active in the lives of the pious ones of ancient Israel. May each encounter with his Word be the opportunity for us to know him better so that we may be effective instruments of his steadfast love in our world. Salvation History continues.

Bibliography

For more detailed treatment and fuller development of the topics included in this book, the reader might consult the following books.

Buttrick, G. A., ed. *The Interpreters' Dictionary of The Bible* (4 vols.) New York: Abingdon Press, 1962; supplementary volume, 1976.

Anderson, B. *Understanding the Old Testament.* Englewood Cliffs, New Jersey: Prentice-Hall, 1975.

Bright, J. *A History of Israel.* Philadelphia: Westminster Press, 1970.

Brown, R., ed. *The Jerome Commentary on the Bible.* Englewood Cliffs, New Jersey: Prentice-Hall, 1968.

Eissfeldt, O. *The Old Testament, an Introduction.* New York: Harper & Row, 1965.

Kuntz, J. *The People of Ancient Israel.* New York: Harper & Row, 1974.

Laymon, C., ed. *The Interpreters' Commentary on the Bible.* New York: Abingdon Press, 1971.

Link, M. *These Stones Will Shout.* Niles, Illinois: Argus Communications, 1975.

West, J. *Introduction to the Old Testament.* New York: Macmillan Co., 1971.

Index

Aaron, 35, 38
Abel, 21–22
Abomination of Desolation, 123
Abraham, 23–27
Absalom, 58
Adonijah, 58
Ahab, 61, 66–68
Ahaz, 77
Ahmoses II, 33
Ai, 49
Albright, W.F., 49
Alexander the Great, 117, 122
allegorical style, 88
Amalekites, 55
Amaziah, 70
Amos, 68–71, 74, 79, 94, 99
Anathoth, 85, 87
Antiochus III, 122
Antiochus IV Epiphanes, 122, 123, 124
Aphek, 55
apocalyptic literature, 100, 124–127
archaeology, 48–49, 51, 55
Ark of the Covenant, 57
Ashurbanipal, 79
Assyria, 61, 62, 74, 75, 77, 79, 80, 82, 83

Baal(s), 50, 61, 66, 67, 72, 73, 81
Babel, tower of, 21–23
Babylon, 21, 76, 82, 83, 85, 87–88, 90, 98, 99
Babylonian Exile, 13, 18, 88–90, 92, 93

Baruch, 86
Bathsheba, 58
Beni Hassan, 29
Bethel
  city of, 49
  shrine at, 61, 69–70
blood
  covenant, 24
  vengeance, 24

Cain, 21–22
Canaan, 9, 24, 43, 44, 47, 48, 49, 50–51, 53, 55, 56, 72–73
Cantical of Canticals, see Song of Songs
Carchemish, battle of, 85
Carmel, Mount, 67–68
cherubim, 21
circumcision, 27, 123
corporate personality, 26
covenant
  with Noah, 22–23
  with Patriarchs, 25, 27
  with Moses, 37, 58, 62, 69, 70, 72, 121
  at Shechem, 50
  New –of Jeremiah, 87–88
creation, 17–23
Cyrus of Persia, 92–94

D. tradition (Deuteronomic), 15–16, 44–45, 47, 51, 96
Dan, (shrine), 61
Daniel, 100, 103, 124–127

· 133 ·

Discussion Guide

CHAPTER ONE SUMMARY

The Old Testament is the foundation for the New Testament. It is a history of God's covenant with the Hebrews and how they respond to his call. It traces the Jewish history from their exodus out of Egypt, their growth as a nation, their eventual downfall and the subsequent power struggle that existed among them until the Romans took control a century before Christ's birth.

The authors of the Old Testament, who were all inspired by God, wrote to various groups of people, in different ways, over a period that spanned centuries. This collection of books has one purpose: to speak the Word of God to his people. This is why Jesus' teachings in the New Testament are a continuation and explanation of the Hebrew scriptures. We must take the words of the Old Testament in context and be inspired to understand their meaning for us today.

Questions

- Explain the meaning of "salvation history" and how it serves to link the Old and New Testaments.
- What is meant by saying the Bible is "divinely inspired? How is inspiration important on the part of the reader?
- How does the Hebrew concept of Torah relate to the covenant between God and man?
- How does the four-sources hypothesis help the reader understand the message of the Hebrew scriptures?

CHAPTER TWO SUMMARY

Much of Genesis is misunderstood because it is approached as an historical or scientific account of the Creation while its theological value is lost. The creation story was probably written during the Babylonian captivity in order to stand in contrast with the Babylonian myths. The Genesis story stands apart from others because of the harmony present between God and man. It also addresses other topics, including marriage, the role of woman and human frailty.

Abraham, Isaac, Jacob and Joseph are presented as "founding father" figures to the Hebrews. They were patriarchs who led these nomadic people by showing a strong and trusting faith in God. The Hebrews themselves gained an identity of being a chosen people through whom God would manifest his love. Joseph is representative of the Hebrew tribes. He faces many setbacks but emerges unharmed because of God's plan for him and his people.

We, too, are called to a similar faith because we are also heirs of God's promises to the patriarchs.

Questions

- How does the Genesis story differ from most ancient myths concerning the creation?
- What is the relationship between God and man in Genesis 1–3? Why does it change?
- What role did the patriarch play in primitive Hebrew society?
- How are Christians, today, "sons of the covenant"?
- In what ways is Joseph a model to the Hebrews?

CHAPTER THREE SUMMARY

The Exodus is the central event of the Hebrew scriptures. Moses was the main figure in this exodus, a man called by God to lead the Hebrews out of slavery in Egypt. Although they weakened at times, the Hebrews understood their special covenant with God and felt his presence in many ways during their trek.

The Passover is symbolic of the Israelite's favored status with God. The feast probably originated, however, before the time of the exodus as a festival commemorating a new harvest season. In contemporary culture, the occasion has become a symbol of man's quest for freedom and parallels the Christian celebration of the Eucharist.

The Book of Leviticus explains the motivation behind the ancient rituals of sacrifice, showing how they were penitential acts which acknowledged God's greatness. The final two books of the Torah reiterate the importance of the covenant between God and man. God's presence among them is constant and his love for them is steadfast even though man's faith is weak.

Questions

- In what ways is God's presence made known to the Hebrews?
- How did the Hebrews view their covenant with God? What were their responsibilities? How was their's a renewal of God's covenant with the patriarchs?
- Explain the symbolism of the contemporary Passover meal. What similarities exist between it and the Christian eucharistic celebration?
- Compare the ideas of atonement and forgiveness in Leviticus and Numbers to the sacrament of reconciliation.

CHAPTER FOUR SUMMARY

The Book of Joshua describes how the Hebrews finally reached the promised land. Although the description of the fall of Jericho was probably exaggerated, Joshua was still a very heroic figure through whom God fulfilled his promise of a new land.

During the 200 years that followed Joshua, Israel was ruled by judges, the most famous of whom was Samson. The young nation seemed to follow a cycle of sinning, followed by God's judgement and wrath, repentance by the people and then deliverance in the person of a judge. The judge remained as long as he was needed and then returned once again to the ranks of the citizenry.

More serious problems, such as the Philistine threat, moved the Israelites to organize a more central government. First Samuel offers conflicting views about whether or not the idea of a monarchy was ordained by God or through a theological mistake. Samuel annointed Saul as the first king, who was successful in turning back the threat. Daniel soon undercut Saul and began to build the country into a power. David's son, Solomon, completed his father's work only to have Israel split by strife. Eventually, the southern half of the country, Judah, was conquered, followed by the subjugation of Israel by Assyria in 722 B.C. The age of the prophets was about to begin.

Questions

- Why are the accounts of the conquests of Jericho and Canaan so detailed and exaggerated? What purpose does this serve?
- What were the conditions in Canaan that helped to foster paganism?

DISCUSSION GUIDE

- How did the changeover to a monarchical style of government result in a more secularized Israel?
- Cite several advantages and disadvantages to having Israel ruled by 1) a judge, 2) a king.

CHAPTER FIVE SUMMARY

The prophets who emerged in Israel in the tenth century B.C. claimed to be appointed by God in order to speak his word to the people. Their messages were usually warnings to a nation which had become unfaithful to the Mosaic law and which was more concerned with performing rituals.

Elijah was extremely devoted to Yahweh and stands as a model of great strength and faith. He rid Israel of paganism which was even practiced by the king and queen. Amos, known as one of the first writing prophets, blamed Israel for her social structure in which the wealthy ignored the poor. Hosea, a native Israelite himself, reiterated the warnings of Amos while stressing God's forgiving nature to those who turn to him. Micah spoke especially for the oppressed poor of his time but also denounced the professional prohpets and public officials as being corrupt and money-hungry.

The prophet Isaiah spoke during a time of tremendous national and international chaos. He said that faith in God rather than in foreign allies would secure Israel's safety. He also foretold the coming of a savior. Zephaniah reinterpreted the words of Amos and Isaiah by telling Judah that her only hope for redemption was with God. Nahum and Habakkuk spoke of God's capabilities to be both powerful in his wrath and merciful in his forgiveness. Jeremiah offered the Judeans in exile hope that a better day would come when they would once again receive God in their hearts. Ezekial, too, spoke during this time and saw the exile as a blessing if it served to renew the Israelite's faith.

Post-exilic prophets such as Haggai, Zechariah, Malachi, Obadiah and Joel saw this period as Israel's best opportunity to renew herself with the covenant and start anew. Instead of dwelling on the past, they looked to the future with hope. The words of the prophets are just as meaningful and applicable today as they were to Israel 3,000 years ago.

Questions

- What was the prophets' message concerning faith and performing rituals?
- Why did the Hebrews worship the Canaanite god, Baal?
- How was Israel's class structure at the time of Amos a cause for her downfall?
- What did Hosea mean by "knowledge of God"?
- What is the "uncompromised hope" that Isaiah promises Israel?
- Explain the paradox present in the Book of Nahum.
- What meaning do the post-exilic prophets find in the adversity which befell Israel? How do they interpret her future?

CHAPTER SIX SUMMARY

The Old Testament books referred to as "The Writings" lack a sense of continuity. They also differ from the books included in the Torah and the Prophets. Six of those in "The Writings" can be considered as Wisdom literature. They concern the individual rather than the community, are more philosophical in language and do not include the salvation history that is such an integral part of the other Old Testament readings.

Proverbs offers prudential wisdom to the young reader in the form of practical and optimistic advice as to how to live a good life. In the Song of Songs, the perfect union of love between man and woman is shown to be a reflection of God's love. The Book of Job expresses the idea that suffering cannot be explained because God's ways are not the way of man. In much the same vain, Ecclesiastes says that God's wisdom cannot be comprehended because man's wisdom is so limited. But Sirach urges the individual never to cease gaining wisdom and not to stop questioning one's faith.

Finally, in Psalms, the sense of community returns as we come in contact with these songs written for group worship. The Psalms relate all aspects of life to the Almighty and reflect many moods from praise to lament.

Questions

- Draw some comparisons between the love of God for the Israelites and the love between husband and wife.
- How were the men of wisdom important to Israel?
- What is the difference between prudential and reflective wisdom?
- "A faith that cannot be intelligently examined will not stand the test of life's dilemmas." What does this mean?

CHAPTER SEVEN SUMMARY

The final books of the Hebrew scriptures were written during a time of great persecution brought on by the Greeks. The books offered hope to a people whose faith was being tested as never before.

The Book of Esther stressed that Jews shouldn't allow the Gentile domination take away their religious identity.

Ruth portrays a pagan woman who joins the Jewish faith. She shows the Hebrews that even a non-Israelite can share in God's love. The Book of Jonah also shows that Yahweh's love is universal and that there is no one we cannot forgive if he or she is truly sorry.

Maccabees is a triumphant story which tells how the Jews overcame the Greek's attempt at hellenization. The Maccabean revolt that restored the Jewish religion is celebrated at Hannukah.

Daniel, the last book of the Old Testament, is an example of apocalyptic literature. It uses visions and symbols understood only by the Jewish faithful so that the Greeks would not oppose it. The author recalls a previous time of persecution and reminds the people that God has never failed them. He forecasts a time when God will reward the loyal and cast away the oppressors. Jesus Christ is the answer to Daniel's vision.

We are heirs to God's covenant with the Israelites. We can become more aware of him in our own life by seeing his presence in the Jews of the Old Testament. We, like the reluctant Jonah, are called to be his witnesses to the world.

Questions

- Why might the message of the Book of Ruth have been hard for the Israelites to accept?
- How is the Book of Maccabees a reconfirmation of the Mosaic covenant?
- What is apocalyptic literature? Why was it easy for the Israelites to misunderstand?
- How is the Resurrection in the New Testament a fulfillment of the Book of Daniel?
- In what ways is Daniel a good link between the Old and New Testaments?

This book was set in VIP Caledonia at
DEKR Corporation, and manufactured
at Offset Paperback Manufacturers.
The designer was Joseph J. Vesely.

HEAR, O ISRAEL
A Guide to the Old Testament

"Father James Leary has, in this book, produced an introduction to the Old Testament that is brief in form but comprehensive in scope. It affords the reader a panoramic view of the Old Testament, from which the Christian Scriptures sprang.

"The Christian who is unfamiliar with the Old Testament is spiritually the poorer for that, is at a loss to understand much of the New Testament and misses the significance of many of the readings used in the liturgy. To supply such a person's need is Father Leary's objective. He succeeds. He is well versed in the sacred writings that detail Salvation History. He conveys his learning simply, clearly and attractively. Under his skillful guidance readers will see not only the continuity of God's loving dealing with his people in antiquity but also the continuation of that process in their own lives today.

"As an aid to mastering the Bible, to greater appreciation of the liturgy and to a more deeply rooted spirituality, Father Leary's book deserves a warm welcome and high praise."

—Msgr. John S. Kennedy, Editor
The Catholic Transcript

FATHER LEARY is Scripture Professor at Saint Thomas Seminary, Bloomfield, Connecticut.

ARENA LETTRES

8 Lincoln Place, Box 219, Waldwick, NJ 07463